Homosexuality and Psychological Functioning

Contemporary Psychology Series
Edward L. Walker, Editor

The frontiers of psychology are advancing—advancing in response to persistent and fundamental social problems, advancing as a result of improved technology in both research and application, advancing through individual creative effort.

Brooks/Cole Publishing Company will make contemporary ideas, research, and applications widely available to students and scholars through the Contemporary Psychology Series.

Psychological Aspects of International Conflict
Ross Stagner, Wayne State University

An Anatomy for Conformity
Edward L. Walker, The University of Michigan
Roger W. Heyns, President, American Council on Education

Delinquent Behavior in an American City
Martin Gold, The University of Michigan

Feminine Personality and Conflict
Judith M. Bardwick, The University of Michigan
Elizabeth Douvan, The University of Michigan
Matina Horner, Harvard University
David Gutmann, The University of Michigan

Roles Women Play: Readings Toward Women's Liberation
Michele Hoffnung Garskof, Quinnipiac College

Homosexuality and Psychological Functioning
Mark Freedman

Homosexuality and Psychological Functioning

Mark Freedman, Ph.D.

Brooks/Cole
Publishing Company

A Division of Wadsworth Publishing Company, Inc.
Belmont, California

L.C. Cat. Card No.: 70-165815
ISBN 0-8185-0023-9
Printed in the United States of America

1 2 3 4 5 6 7 8 9 10– 75 74 73 72 71

12-86

This book was edited by Konrad Kerst and designed
by Linda Marcetti. The cover photograph is by Mike
Powers. The book was typeset at Design Service, Fullerton,
California, and printed and bound at Hamilton Printing
Company, Rensselaer, New York.

"We realize that every good thing dates, and grasp better the complexities of life's compensations."

Wyndham Lewis,
The Caliph's Design

Preface

Homosexuality, formerly a taboo topic, has moved from social untouchability to scientific enquiry, and it is now possible to investigate and discuss this phenomenon rationally. I believe that homosexuality is an area of interest in any country in which it exists: its pervasiveness extends from America to Australia, from Scandinavia to South Africa.

This book seeks to ascertain the relationship between homosexual behavior and psychological functioning. The first chapter deals very generally with prevalent attitudes and approaches to homosexual behavior in our society. The other chapters expand the discussions introduced in Chapter 1, examine fallacies in current attitudes toward adjustment and normality, and present the surprising results of research studies on the psychological functioning of homosexually oriented individuals.

Throughout this book I present the disguised biographies of persons who are representative of the homosexual population. These are real people, whom I am describing to the best of my ability as a trained observer and psychologist. These individuals were indirectly contacted through homosexual groups. They agreed to be interviewed and to take psychological tests in order to aid in the progress of this book; my understanding with them was that I would ensure their anonymity by disguising demographic data which would identify them and that I would provide them with feedback about their performances on the psychological tests if they wanted it. Their motivations for participating in this endeavor ranged from an interest in changing the societal image of homosexuality to personal curiosity about psychological tests and about their own functioning as evaluated by a psychologist.

I wrote this book from my background as an American psychologist who holds an optimistic outlook about human adaptability. Happily, I am finding that this attitude is shared by many educated, socially involved people throughout the world and am hopeful that this book will be interesting and meaningful to them.

I want to thank the Daughters of Bilitis for their participation in my research and for their help in sending me journal articles when I was out of reach of good library facilities. I was fortunate to have a Harvard Ph.D. in English Literature, Jerry Lutz, help me with grammar and style; any errors in syntax, therefore, must be attributed to poor training at America's oldest university. Florence Conrad of the D.O.B. and David Ivison of the University of Sydney Clinical Psychology Unit read the manuscript for content, as did Edward L. Walker of the University of Michigan. I am grateful for their useful suggestions.

The ideas of my teachers George W. Albee and Frederick Herzberg stimulated my thinking on new approaches to normality and good psychological functioning. And I received useful feedback from my students in Cleveland, Tokyo, Bangkok, and Sydney, who did not hesitate to question me about any ambiguity or unsupported hypothesis. Research funds from the University of Sydney enabled me to revise the manuscript of the book.

The Brooks/Cole staff—especially Terry Hendrix, Jean Strieff, and Konrad Kerst—have helped me tremendously in preparing the book for publication. And my typists, Bette Thornton and Eleanor Sallos, did a beautiful job of converting semi-legible handwriting to ultra-neat manuscript.

Finally, for ego support along the way I must thank Erv Polster, Marty Rogers, and my parents—friends indeed.

I dedicate this book to the memory of my friend and teacher Mildred Weiss.

Mark Freedman

Contents

Homosexuality and Psychological Functioning

1

Homosexuality
Today

Homosexuality is coming to be recognized as a major social concern and behavioral phenomenon. It has been conservatively estimated that in the United States alone there are at least four million men and one million women whose predominant (or exclusive) interpersonal sexual relations are with members of their own sex (Cory, 1964). Also, homosexuality is a *pervasive* phenomenon—it is found in virtually all infrahuman species, in all strata of human society, and in all geographical areas. Even if it were not so prominent or pervasive, homosexuality as a psychosocial phenomenon would still be an important topic to study.

Until recently, homosexuality was regarded almost exclusively in terms of morality. Only within the last few decades has it been considered from other perspectives—genetic, physiological, sociological, and psychological. The latter two perspectives seem the most promising in giving us a clearer understanding of the basis of homosexuality and of the consequences to the personal adjustment of the individual.

Many scholars have asserted that homosexuality has been present since man evolved. Eric Dingwall suggests that homosexuality is as old as humanity itself. He holds that examples of homosexuality have been recorded from the earliest times and noted among a great range of peoples. The fact that it occurs in primitive peoples as well as in advanced cultures indicates that it is not the result of cultural decay or degeneration, as many people like to believe (1961, page 42).

Certainly homosexuality among both males and females is described (or alluded to) in some of the best-known literature in the world. The Hebrew scriptures refer to homosexual practices in highly negative terms; this is prototypic of the Judaic and Christian traditions of regarding homosexuality as sinful and as demanding of punishment.

On the other hand, Sappho described love among women in delicate and touching verses. (From Sappho, one of the best lyric poets ever known, come the terms "sapphic" and "lesbian.") Plato's *Symposium,* written about 380 B.C., equates homosexuality with the finest love man is capable of; he proposed these relations as a means of attaining man's yearning after the beautiful. And Shakespeare wrote some of his most enduring sonnets to a young man. He also created many situations in his comedies where, because of disguised identities, homosexuality is clearly implied.

The author most associated with homosexuality in the public mind, Oscar Wilde, suggested the more sordid side of "the love which dare not speak its name" in his novel *The Picture of Dorian Gray.* His personal life was both more colorful and more sordid than his writings: it was his sexual preferences and his flamboyance that brought the wrath of Victorian England on him.

Radclyffe Hall's classic novel about Lesbianism, *The Well of Loneliness,* is a powerful depiction of the direct and covert pressures against homosexuality in Western societies. Homosexuality is also the theme of many recent novels and plays by such authors as James Baldwin, Tennessee Williams, Lillian Hellman, Jean Genet, Christopher Isherwood, Gore Vidal, Mary Renault, John Rechy, Matt Crowley, Charles Dyer, Jean Paul Sartre, James Purdy, Frank Marcus, and Robert Anderson. These plays and novels range from Genet's bizarre but enlightening masturbation fantasies in prison (*Our Lady of the Flowers*) to the sensitively written story of the aging college professor who has experienced joy and frustration because of his homosexual orientation (Isherwood's *A Single Man*). Since each of these works investigates a valid but specific aspect of "the gay life," no one work could be said to be a description of the totality, or *gestalt*, or even to be the most accurate representation of this world. Some of the aspects of homosexuality that these authors treat are the pleasures of homoerotic sex; the quest for identity; the guilt, shame and self-doubt; the ironic, witty humor; the ever-present threat of blackmail; the suppression of genuine emotions and potentialities; the search for "true love" and the settling for superficial displays of affection; and the dogged—and sometimes courageous—attempts to survive despite persistent stress and problems of living.

As suggested above, there have been varying attitudes toward homosexuality in different societies and cultures. In Western societies, at least since the reign of the Roman emperor Justinian, the official societal attitude and posture toward homosexuality has been condemnatory, and punitive as well. This attitude has not succeeded in eliminating homosexual activities; it has merely made them less visible.

The sanctions that society wields against individuals practicing homosexual relations include legal, psychological, and social ones. Especially in America, there is tremendous overt agression (in the form of beatings) and implicit violence (such as threats and gossip) directed against homosexually oriented persons. It is amazing how quickly most people will write off an individual when they discover his homosexual orientation, regardless of his intellectual or social assets. (This is done despite our professed claim that every citizen is entitled to his right to live his life however he wants, so long as he does not interfere with the freedom of others.) Homosexuality is considered to be a sexual "inversion," "perversion," and "deviation." Individuals who engage in homosexual behavior are seen alternatively as being immature, immoral, or ill. Nevertheless, these attitudes and sanctions have resulted not in the elimination of homosexuality as a sexual outlet but only in its seeming disappearance: that is, the pressures against homosexuality have caused the behavior to go underground, and individuals who engage in this behavior in Western society have, by and large, taken on the mask of heterosexuality in their everyday dealings with the outside world, much as many Jews—the Marranos—disguised themselves as Christians during the Spanish Inquisition.

An example of a homosexually oriented person who appears to the outside world to be heterosexual is shown in the biography of James Carter below.

James Carter

James Carter is a 31-year-old sales manager of a large Detroit-based company that manufactures plastics. He is a White Anglo-Saxon Protestant, the youngest of four sons of English immigrant parents. After graduation from college (where he first accepted and acted on his homosexual impulses), he enlisted in the military. During his time in the military, he had heterosexual and homosexual experiences. He joined his present company immediately after his discharge from the service, when he was 26. His sales manager's job and his salary allow him to travel with great frequency, mostly within the United States (to company branch offices and dealerships) and occasionally to the foreign branch offices of his company in Canada and Panama. Carter's intelligence, as measured by the Wechsler Adult Intelligence Scale, is in the "bright normal" range. His interests are wide-ranging, his tastes catholic. A subscriber to about 15 magazines and newspapers, Carter also enjoys reading history and biographies. He prides himself on being in touch with what's happening in the world; with respect to technological and social changes in the world, his pride in his knowledge is justified.

Carter, having had enjoyable experience with both homosexual and heterosexual sexuality, now is predisposed to homosexual outlets for his sexual needs. He is moderately handsome, very much the business type in his personal appearance and mannerisms, an individual who would not be recognized as homosexually oriented. Carter, like most pragmatic homosexually oriented people, maintains the facade of heterosexuality in most of his dealings. Even in homosexual situations, such as at bars or parties, he is reluctant to give his full name, for the consequences of his sexual orientation becoming known to his boss would mean immediate dismissal, despite his acknowledged competence on his job. (He even admits that, given the nature of the stereotypes about homosexuality, his subordinates would no longer respect him if his sexual orientation were known.)

Carter is a sociable person, one who knows how to present himself well in gay bars and at homosexual parties in order to make sexual and social contacts. He is primarily attracted to collegiate-looking men and other clean-cut types, and disdains the effeminacy which is sometimes manifested by homosexually oriented people. The sexual behaviors he engages in are passive partnership in fellatio,* active partnership in anal intercourse, body rubbing and mutual masturbation, and, occasionally, passive partnership in anal intercourse. He feels that, for him, the sexual foreplay is often as enjoyable—or even more enjoyable—than the sexual acts themselves.

Although Carter has sexual relations with a comparatively large number of people, perhaps four or five a month, he has established a long-term relationship with one person whom he likes and respects. This friend does not live with him, but they travel together and enjoy social activities such as going to dinner and the theater. Although they frequently have sex together, they also have an understanding that it is permissible for each of them to have sex with other people. This arrangement obviates the need for duplicity and the possibility of extreme jealousy or resentment. (They both believe that men were not created as monogamous creatures in regard to sexual situations.) Carter's friend is, like himself, a

---

*See Chapter 2 for clarifying descriptions of these and other sexual practices.

businessman who takes an interest in many aspects of living. He is a graduate of an Ivy-League college and an estimable school of business as well.

Carter, when he first acknowledged his homosexual urges in college, was ashamed of them. He has now come to terms with his homosexual interests, believing them to be a natural and valid expression of his sexuality; he admits the inconvenience of his sexual orientation, but to him the pleasure and excitement he derives from sexual experiences with men are preferable to heterosexual experiences and outweigh the inconvenience of hiding his sexual orientation from the world. Carter is generally happy with his life situation. He is caught up with his work and is growing in his competence as a sales manager and in his proficiency in interacting with people. His basic needs, such as those for sex, companionship, status, and money, are well taken care of. Carter's performance on psychological tests is consonant with this appraisal of his functioning: he obtained a low score on a measure of neuroticism, achieved a relatively high score on extraversion, and showed normal to self-actualizing behavior on other measures of psychological functioning.

There is a direct correspondence between the interpretation of a phenomenon such as homosexuality and the consequent actions taken toward it. For example, some sexologists including Magnus Hirschfeld, Krafft-Ebing, and Havelock Ellis have argued that since homosexuality is either inborn or the result of hormonal imbalance, the "homosexual" cannot be held accountable for his condition or his behavior and thus should not be punished. On the other hand, when homosexuality has been viewed as voluntary, immoral sexual behavior, legal measures have been created to deal with it. Probably the most widespread view of homosexuality currently held is that it is a sexual deviation which is indicative of personality disturbance or of "mental illness." Typical of this approach is the conclusion of an extensive psychoanalytic study by Bieber and associates:

In our view, the human has a capacity for homosexuality but a tendency toward heterosexuality. The capacity for responsivity to heterosexual excitation is inborn—courtship behavior and copulatory technique is learned. Homosexuality, on the other hand, is acquired and discovered as a circumventive adaptation for coping with fear of heterosexuality ... We do not hold with the now popular thesis that in all adult males there are repressed homosexual wishes. In fact, most adult heterosexual males no longer have the potential for a homosexual adaption. ... If we assume that homosexuality is a pathological condition, and our data strongly support this assumption, we would no more expect latent homosexuality to be inevitable among well-integrated heterosexuals than we would expect latent peptic ulcers to be inevitable among all members of a healthy population [1962, page 305].

Of course, the consequent action usually taken against a pathological condition is to try to treat it; that is what has happened with homosexuality. There are various types of therapy being used, and it may be helpful to look at some of them briefly.

Psychiatrists, and particularly psychoanalysts, have viewed homosexuality as a disease and as a manifestation of fear of the opposite sex. Their "treatment" of individuals who have engaged in homosexual behavior has been based on working through the fear of the opposite sex, often centering around the "unresolved Oedipus Complex"—the patient's sexual feelings toward his mother, supposedly antecedent to, and analogous to, his sexual feeling toward all other females. Representative of the results of psychoanalytic psychotherapy in "curing" individuals who engage in homosexual relations is the data from the Bieber study:

Of 106 homosexuals who undertook psychoanalysis, either as exclusively homosexual or bisexual, 29 (27 per cent) became exclusively heterosexual. Only 2 patients of 28 (7 per cent) who had fewer than 150 hours became heterosexual . . . Eighteen of 38 (47 per cent) of those patients who had 350 or more hours of analysis became heterosexual [1962, page 301].

Albert Ellis has had a similar lack of success with his early "psychoanalytically oriented" psychotherapy and his more recent "rational-emotive" psychotherapy with individuals who engage in homosexual behavior. He believes that therapeutic success with "homosexuals" is due to the specific strategy of the therapist. One must accept the "homosexual's" desires and acts but be critical of neurotic motivations. The emphasis should be on the patient becoming *more* heterosexual rather than less homosexual. The patient's sense of guilt and shame about sex (as well as other irrational ideas about it) must be attacked. Emphasis should be placed on ego-strengthening and feelings of adequacy. Heterosexual relationships should be encouraged (Ellis, 1963).

Another prominent therapy for homosexuality has been the recent "behavior therapy." Behavior therapists take the position that virtually all human behavior is learned and can be modified through the use of the proper reward or punishment. Behavior that is considered to be the product of psychological disturbance is essentially learned maladaptive behavior and can be changed using appropriate conditioning techniques. Behavior therapy assumes two objectives in treating homosexual behavior: the first is the elimination of homoerotic behavior, and the second is the eliciting or increasing of heterosexual behavior in the person's behavioral repertoire. The first objective has been dealt with using such measures as coupling homosexual thoughts and fantasies with emetics, electric shock, and other aversive conditions; measures taken toward the second objective include desensitization procedures and the appearance of heterosexual stimuli with the termination of electric shock (thus pairing these stimuli with relief from anxiety). It is certainly questionable whether one should *create* anxiety in one area of sexuality while concurrently trying to *diminish* it in another area. The

behavior therapists have confined their treatment of homosexuality to artificial, laboratory experiences, since they have
been unable to deal with the real-life stimulus situations
directly. They have hoped that laboratory learning would
"generalize" (transfer) to real-life contexts—something that
usually does not happen, as most learning theorists and
psychotherapists are well aware. Behavior therapy for homosexuality has been done with a very limited number of cases,
and there is, so far, a dearth of adequate follow-up studies on
the "cures."

There have been other approaches to homosexu-
ality by behavioral scientists. A recent one, evolving out of a
psychological study by Evelyn Hooker (1957), suggests these
tentative conclusions: homosexuality as a clinical entity does
not exist—it is as varied as the forms of heterosexuality;
homosexuality may be a deviation in sexual pattern which is
within the normal range psychologically; and the role of
particular forms of sexual desire and expression in personality structure may be less important than has been frequently assumed. Of course, the implication of this approach
is that if homosexuality is not necessarily a manifestation of
psychopathology, then there is no reason to try to "treat" it,
modify it, or eliminate it on psychological grounds. The
biography of Grace Schilling below illustrates this perspective
on sexuality.

Grace Shilling

Grace Schilling is a 52-year-old executive
secretary for a medium-sized Pittsburgh investment
firm. She is a Roman Catholic, one who is able to
reconcile her religious beliefs with her sexual
orientation. Grace was the oldest of five children,
four of whom are still alive. She was married to a
high school teacher for twenty years. After his
death twelve years ago, which was an unexpected
and painful experience for her, she lived alone for
three years. She disliked living alone but did not
feel up to dating or remarriage. About two years
after her husband's death, her money began to run
out, and she took a secretarial job in the

investment firm where she now works. (Prior to her marriage, she had earned a degree at a business school and had worked for two years as a clerk-typist.) During this period, she met a woman who was interested, as Grace was, in sharing a place. Grace offered to rent her a room in her house, which the woman accepted. After living several months in the house, the woman told Grace about her homosexual orientation and convinced Grace to have sexual relations with her. The sexual experiences were pleasurable to Grace, and she has continued to engage in homosexual relations since then, for the arrangement between the woman and herself fulfills her needs for companionship as well as sexuality. The sexual acts that Grace engages in are mutual fondling, mutual masturbation, and passive partnership in cunnilingus. (She finds these sexual behaviors different from those she engaged in with her husband but fully as satisfactory.)

Grace has been executive secretary in the investment firm for three years, having been given more and more challenging and interesting assignments in her ten years with the company. As executive secretary, she has much responsibility; although she is not paid commensurately with this responsibility, she earns enough money to support herself. She has amicable relationships with the other people in the firm, but she does not disclose anything about her private life except that she is a widow.

On the Wechsler Adult Intelligence Scale, Grace achieved an intelligence quotient in the "superior" range. She did particularly well on the parts of this test involved with verbal and mathematical facility, as well as with the parts measuring "social comprehension." Grace scored low on measures of neuroticism and extraversion, and in the normal range on the scales of another personality inventory. (She scored high, however, on measures of inner-direction, existentiality, and feeling reactivity.) Grace seems to be able to transcend the artificial dichotomies prevalent in society, the either-or categories such as "masculine -feminine" and "moral-immoral." Her functioning can be characterized as average or better and as occasionally manifesting traits characteristic of self-actualizing people.

Grace Schilling is happy with her life now. She accepts her present life as calmly and assuredly as she looks back on her years with her husband. And she believes in the value of human life in general, as well as in the pleasure of living.

It should be obvious that with the diversity of opinions about the meaning and consequences of homosexuality for an individual, there is a felt need for good psychological research that will assess the relevant psychological aspects of the phenomenon, and for a clear framework in which to fit this research. This book attempts to bring to light the psychological research on homosexuality (including some studies previously unreported) and to fit this research into a viable theory of the relationship between homosexuality and psychological functioning. There will be no attempt made, however, to delineate the fullness of the topic of homosexuality. Hundreds of writers have investigated the nuances of heterosexuality without exhausting the possibilities: the same richness of material is true for homosexuality, a richness that surely cannot be encompassed in one book.

2

Homosexual Terms
and Practices

A Behavioral Definition of Homosexuality

There are many different ways of defining homosexuality. For the purposes of this book, homosexuality will
be operationally defined as sexual relations between members of the same sex. This definition is justifiable and
meritorious on a number of grounds. First of all, the only
objective way we can judge a behavioral phenomenon is in
behavioral terms. This, as many prominent behaviorists have
pointed out, is due to the need to be concerned with directly
observable events:

In psychology one is concerned with the
problem of terminology at every stage, but particularly when one seems to be getting away from
directly observable events. When we talk about
behavior we mean that which man does: the
walking, talking, swimming; the being anxious or
bright or loyal, and so on, that is observed in men
and that behavioral scientists are interested in
describing and explaining. The terms "anxious,"
"bright" and "loyal," however, may not appear to
refer to observable behavior in the same way as do

"walking," "talking" and "swimming." Nevertheless, as long as these former terms are thought of as
nothing more than "shorthand" labels for classes
of behavior—"anxious" behavior, "loyal" behavior,
and so on—we are on safe ground. Unfortunately,
in everyday thinking, people commonly act as if
the "real" thing to study is not the behavior itself,
but rather some inner entity, "anxiety" or
"loyalty," which accounts for the behavior
observed. Many times, however, no such inferred
inner entity is adequately specified by observation.
Thus, such an approach may violate a basic
scientific dictum that the events of interest must
be observable by any investigator sufficiently
trained to observe them [Staats, 1964, page 12].

Specifically, the main alternative to viewing homosexuality as sexual *behavior* is to talk about homosexual
desire. The problem in talking about sexual desire is that it
generally has to be *inferred* from some type of behavior—
either from actual sexual behavior or from verbal reports of
feelings about another person. (Psychotherapists, of course,
often infer homosexual desire from some more remote
behavior, such as from dreams or fantasies reported by
inhibited individuals; the basis for such interpretations,
however, is still *behavioral.*)

One qualification of this definition is necessary
here. To define homosexuality in behavioral terms is not to
imply that this sexual outlet has the same meaning for every
individual who uses it, that there is the same quality of
personality functioning in all persons who engage in homosexual behavior, or that we will find the same social-learning
experiences in their backgrounds. However, the ultimate
choice of sexual outlets does appear to be determined by
social-learning experiences: that is, sexual behavior is dependent on the individual's past direct and indirect (symbolic)
experiences with various sexual stimuli. For example, a man
would be sexually responsive toward other men if he had
positive, rewarding sexual experiences with his peers during
adolescence. However, if these experiences were aversive to
him or if he had been deeply imbued with societal taboos

against homosexual behavior, then men would not be sexually stimulating to him, or homosexuality a likely sexual outlet. Note that the term "social learning" does not necessarily imply that these behaviors and attitudes are *consciously* acquired. Learning psychologists have demonstrated repeatedly that emotional responses, attitudinal postures, and other diverse preferences can be conditioned without the subject's knowledge or specific consent. In other words, a person's sexual-behavior pattern is learned and is subject to the orderly laws of acquisition and extinction that govern virtually all behavior. Clarence Tripp (1965) maintains that there are fundamental similarities between homosexuality and heterosexuality: "Not the least of these are its origins in learning processes, and the tenacity with which it is capable of staying put against the moralistic opposition that has been brought against it from time to time" (page 22).

It must be emphasized here that this sexual-behavior pattern is not established through one unique experience; it is multidetermined. To view homosexuality as sexual behavior is not to suggest that the motives surrounding the behavior are only sexual. Homosexuality may at times be merely a means of sexual gratification, but as with heterosexuality it is more often involved with needs central to the individual's personality, such as the need for companionship, love, dependency, or the "will to power." There are often non-sexual motives behind homosexual behavior: this, however, does not obviate the fact that the only objective way to examine homosexuality is in behavioral terms, as a sexual outlet.

Also, the use of the word "homosexual" as a noun will be avoided as much as possible. The dichotomy of "homosexuals" and "heterosexuals" is highly artificial because man is inherently a *pansexual* creature, capable of responding to a variety of sexual stimuli. Tripp contends that every sexually responsive person could respond to every other sexually responsive individual if it weren't for aversion reactions (1965, page 20). In fact, shifts in sexual preference and sexual outlet often occur within an individual's lifetime. Thus, labeling the person a "homosexual" or "heterosexual" implies a permanent, irreversible pattern of preference and behavior that is not substantiated by available evidence. (Many psychologists have noted the depersonalizing effect of labeling an individual. This dehumanizing effect may be particularly pronounced with already disturbed persons, where the label—or diagnosis—sometimes stereotypes these persons for life.) Also, the noun "homosexual" has become a pejorative, and it is a stigma for the person who is assigned this title. The flaw in labels such as "homosexual" and "heterosexual" is shown in the biography of William Buckner below.

William Buckner

William Buckner is a 27-year-old sales representative for an Indianapolis-based building supplies firm. He is the second child of six children (four boys and two girls); his parents are Roman Catholic. Buckner's education was obtained in church schools: he graduated from a Catholic parochial high school and from a Jesuit college. He had sporadic heterosexual experiences when he was in high school and college; after graduation from college, he steadily dated one girl, whom he subsequently married. They now have three children. About two years after he married, Buckner discovered his homosexual urges. Subsequently, during business trips around the country, he started finding sexual partners in gay bars. These experiences were pleasurable to him, and he has continued to engage in these activities when he is on the road. He has admitted his homosexual interests to his wife, their marriage being a truthful and open relationship. She—chiefly because of her Roman Catholic upbringing—is bothered by this, but she still feels very close to her husband and wants to maintain their marriage. They have come to an implicit understanding that as long as he does not discuss these homosexual activities or engage in them in their city, she will accept this aspect of his life. Their own sexual relationship is still satisfactory to them, and they have sexual relations about every other day when he is home. (His job entails traveling from ten to twenty days a month.) Buckner now avails himself of the short stays in different cities to find sexual partners for between one and three days. He is fairly successful at this, since he is pleasant looking, although not really handsome. The sexual behaviors he engages in are mutual masturbation, active or passive partnership in fellatio, and active partnership in anal intercourse. He finds homosexual activities frequently more stimulating than heterosexual relations, although the latter behaviors are also enjoyable to him, and he and his wife are not rigid in their choice of sexual behavior (that is, they do not restrict themselves to face-to-face intercourse).

Buckner trusts himself, in that he trusts his feelings, interests, and ideas. He was able to assimilate his homosexual urges because of this, making them an integral part of his life. The same adjustments are true of his career: at two points in his work background he has taken a risk in changing jobs, and both times they were the right decisions and advanced him considerably in salary and professional competence. He is open to new experience, and although slightly wary of change (as most of us are) he welcomes challenge and growth opportunities. In this regard, he sees his homosexual activities as enhancing his life rather than detracting from it.

Buckner obtained an intelligence quotient in the "bright normal" range on the Wechsler Adult Intelligence Scale. His strengths in this test were in the areas of mathematical facility, general knowledge, and visual abstraction. On personality tests, his performance was characterized by lack of disturbance in psychological functioning, as well as by traits of extraversion, inner-directedness, and existentiality. He also demonstrated remarkable "tolerance for ambiguity," as well as high self-acceptance and self-regard. From the viewpoints of social, sexual, and work experience, Buckner's functioning could only be described as positive and fulfilling.

The terms "homosexual" and "heterosexual" are not used in this book except in quoting other authors who still use this dichotomy. Instead, the terms "homosexually oriented individual" and "heterosexually oriented individual" are used, mainly to avoid the exclusive implications of the former terms. A "homosexually oriented individual" is a person whose interpersonal sexual experiences are predominantly with members of his own sex, although this does not preclude his having sexual experiences with members of the opposite sex also. Similarly, a "heterosexually oriented individual" is a person whose interpersonal sexual experiences are predominantly with members of the opposite sex, although this does not preclude occasional sexual experiences with members of his own sex. (The term "interpersonal sexual experiences" is used throughout the book to distinguish between sexual behaviors that involve another person and those that do not—principally, individual masturbation, an autoerotic sexual behavior that is technically the most frequently used sexual outlet of all.)

Sexual Practices

Psychological functioning is inextricably related to sexual practices, particularly because of the influence of these practices on self-concept and social acceptance. There is considerable confusion about what homosexually oriented men and women actually do in bed. Misinformation and stereotypes about these sexual activities abound. Since it seems useful to the subject matter in this book to provide clarifying descriptions of sexual practices and their social and psychological implications, this chapter includes separate sections on the sexual practices of homosexually oriented men and women, with emphasis on typical patterns and characteristic responses.

Sex Among Men

There are many ways in which homosexual behavior may emerge in a given individual. Sometimes a homosexual experience precedes the person's identification of himself as a "homosexual"; more often, this self-concept (based on his interest, desires, mannerisms, and social role) leads to increasingly frequent homosexual experience. In both cases—especially the latter—initial sexual practices are limited; inexperience and feelings of guilt or shame militate against the beginner. These initial activities often include simple kissing (rather than "French" kissing) and mutual masturbation (in which each manipulates the genitals of his partner to orgasm).

As the person gains more sexual experience, differentiated sexual activities and definite preferences arise. Sexual activities among men generally have certain preliminaries: there is usually fondling, massaging, open-mouth kissing, and other sexually arousing techniques. After this, there are several typical patterns—fellatio, body rubbing, mutual masturbation, and anal intercourse.

Fellatio is the technique by which one person brings another to orgasm through oral manipulation of the penis. The adoption of this practice often involves concomitant shame and guilt and necessitates some reorganization of the person's self-concept because of the stereotypes equated with this sexual activity.

Body rubbing is a sexual activity among men which, along with kissing and fondling, arouses the partners and sometimes results in orgasm. This is an unsatisfactory activity for many homosexually oriented men unless a sexual lubricant is used to decrease the friction between the bodies and to increase the pleasurable sensations.

Anal intercouse involves the insertion of the penis of one partner into the other's anus. Many homosexually oriented men find this painful and unpleasant (either from the active or the passive role) because of the physical strain that exists; others find the activity depersonalizing, because they feel they are treating their partner like an object.

There are also less frequent activities among men. It is difficult to estimate how widespread these practices are. One of them is a variation of fellatio: "around the world." In this activity, the fellator moves his tongue around the groin to the anus. The thought of this practice is aversive to many homosexually oriented men; however, it is said to be highly arousing and pleasurable for the passive partner.

Another sexual activity among men is multiple sex among three or more people. Various combinations of fellation, body rubbing, mutual masturbation, and anal intercourse occur in multiple sex. Often, one person is being fellated by another while he is the passive recipient of the penis of the third person in either fellatio or anal intercourse. Occasionally, six to ten people engage in an orgy in which all sorts of sexual activities happen simultaneously, augmented by alcohol, drugs, and sexual lubricants. Multiple sex, however, is probably no more common among homosexually oriented persons than it is among heterosexually oriented ones.

Sado-masochistic sexual activity is another relatively infrequent practice in the homosexual sphere. The sadist derives intense pleasure from inflicting pain and from subjecting another person to his will. The masochist, conversely, takes pleasure in being hurt or in being dominated and humiliated. Often, sado-masochistic activities involve whips, ropes, or other devices to inflict pain; sometimes, domination (without special devices) is sufficient to give pleasure. Of course, sado-masochistic practices occur not only in homosexual situations but in heterosexual ones as well; the term "sadist" derives from the Marquis de Sade, a French nobleman who wrote of elaborate tortures of women by men in *Justine* and other books.

Physical objects are sometimes used to augment homosexual arousal or climax. One such object is the "beefcake" magazine, containing photos of nude young men with semi-erect penises (it is illegal to sell magazines with photos of fully-aroused men). The poses and stories are as diverse as in "cheesecake" publications. Less readily available than "beefcake" magazines are hard-core pornographic photos, which show young men performing all kinds of sexual acts together.

To improve the quality of an orgasm, some homosexually oriented men use "poppers" (isoamyl nitrite)—prescription capsules that are broken and inhaled immediately before a climax to heighten and extend it. These are used infrequently, especially since the use of marijuana has become commonplace. Marijuana increases the sensuality of most activities, including sex: the tactile sensations are especially heightened.

How do homosexually oriented men find sexual partners? There are many ways, including "gay" bars, restaurants, parks, turkish baths, and beaches. The closest analogue to a gay bar in the heterosexual world is a singles or "Friday" bar, where men pick up young women. In a gay bar, homosexually oriented men meet each other in an atmosphere conducive to picking up someone as well as to ordinary socializing with friends and acquaintances. In some bars, dancing between men is allowed (the laws are variable on this, and sometimes fast dancing is permissible but not slow, body-contact dancing). The possibility of meeting someone new and attractive always pervades these bars. Some men use gay bars solely for the function of finding a sexual partner; others enjoy the relaxed atmosphere and friendliness of the bar and do not actively seek sexual partners. People who frequent gay bars quickly learn how to make themselves as sexually attractive to others as possible. Generally, this means looking youthful, masculine, well-groomed, and collegiate (although there are certain bars in which looking tough or far-out is rewarded). Often, the people in the bar look a little too right, too perfect (every hair in place and kept there with hairspray) or as though they have cultivated a studied casualness. (Hence the line from *The Boys in the Band*: "One thing about masturbation, at least you don't have to look your best.") Sometimes, the atmosphere of the bar clearly emphasizes picking up a sexual partner (like some heterosexual singles bars); many people feel like an object or "piece of meat on a hook" in this situation. Pickups often begin with one person staring at or standing near the person he's attracted to; a conversation is begun by one of them; and it is quickly apparent by the interest or disinterest of each whether there is a mutual sexual attraction. Often, the two go home to have sex within an hour of the initial meeting. Sometimes, these pickups become long-term sexual affairs or friendships; often, they are just "one-night stands."

Besides bars, there are homosexual restaurants (because of their clientele or staff), parks, and beaches. In these places, homosexually oriented men "cruise" one another (use verbal or non-verbal communication for a pickup). Homosexually oriented men are often recognizable to each other on the street, in a park, or on a beach by subtle cues they give each other. Probably the most common cue is prolonged eye contact, where two people will maintain a gaze much longer than is typical of social interaction. Also, where the eyes are directed in another cue: homosexually oriented men often look at a man's face and then let their gaze descend to the man's crotch in "that telling 45° angle." Cruising is a commonplace and relatively harmless homosexual activity (it is unobtrusive to most people).

Another, more blatant homosexual meeting place is the homosexual turkish bath. This is a situation in which men can have casual, impersonal sex. Men meet each other in the hallways, steamrooms, and shower rooms of the baths and have sex in their private rooms or in the more public steamrooms. Every major city has a homosexual turkish bath.

Less frequent than people think is the use of public toilets for homosexual meeting places. These are dangerous because the homosexually oriented male may misread cues and try to pick up an unwilling person or else a plainclothesman trying to entrap him. For most homosexually oriented men, public toilets as pickup places are aversive and not a real option.

There is homosexual prostitution, different in many ways from the heterosexual kind. Male prostitutes, hustlers, and "models" sometimes walk around the streets and parks waiting to be picked up (as in the 42nd Street scene in *Midnight Cowboy*) but just as often they frequent certain bars or advertise in underground newspapers such as *The Berkeley Barb*. The male prostitutes almost invariably emphasize their masculinity and physical endowments ("well hung stud, great in bed"): their sexual practices are generally active partnership in anal intercourse or passive partnership in fellatio—activities considered more masculine or "butch." Typically, their patrons are older men who otherwise have difficulty in finding sexual partners.

Sex among men is thus diverse and varied, as are the contexts in which men meet other men for sexual encounters. In our society, men are encouraged to have many sexual conquests; this outlook is shared by both homosexually and heterosexually oriented men. Differing social conventions make brief sexual encounters more likely in the homosexual world: there is less need for extended dating or professions of love in order to set up a sexual encounter than in heterosexual situations. Also, there are no formal social arrangements such as marriage to sustain a homosexual relationship. These factors, along with the clandestine atmosphere of homosexual meeting places, create the promiscuity or casualness of sex among men. However, within the homosexual world there are strong codes of morality and acceptable behavior that require discretion, secrecy, and personal responsibility to sexual partners. For instance, imposing one's will on another person without his consent is regarded much the same way as rape is in the heterosexual world; also, even more than in the heterosexual world, secrecy and discretion about the identity of sexual partners is mandatory. Thus, even though the homosexual world does not follow the accepted heterosexual social and legal conventions, homosexual activities do occur within a strong ethical and moral context.

Sex Among Women

Men in our culture put much emphasis on sexual conquest; women, on long-term emotional relationships. This is as true for homosexually oriented women as for heterosexually oriented ones: *sex* is secondary to *emotion*.

A typical pattern of "coming out" (gradual acknowledgement of sexual interest) for a homosexually oriented woman is an early (often one-sided) emotional attachment to another female. This generally occurs in the woman's late teens or early twenties; she discovers strong feelings of warmth, tenderness, or love toward another woman. This discovery produces confusion and disturbance; often, the course of action is to turn away from the situation and its new, unprecedented feelings. Five or six years later, emotional attraction to another woman may be accompanied by sexual feelings; this may also cause the woman to run away from the implications of her feelings, but it may be the start of her identification as a "Lesbian." With this identification, the woman may seek out others of her kind. (Sometimes, the woman may try out heterosexual sex and even marriage before she ascertains that she is attracted primarily to woman.) Generally, homosexual identification precedes actual sexual behavior; sexual experimentation before self-identification as homosexual is rare among women, and seduction by another woman as the first step is even rarer. After a woman "comes out" in the homosexual world, her initial sexual practices are generally limited to passive partnership in various activities. There are two typical sexual practices among homosexually oriented woman—cunnilingus and mutual masturbation—and one less frequent activity, tribadism.

Cunnilingus is analogous to fellatio. In it, the active partner moves her tongue down the body of the other (after considerable fondling, kissing, and other foreplay) until she reaches the clitoris. By oral manipulation she brings her partner to orgasm. Mutual cunnilingus is relatively infrequent, although sometimes one partner performs cunnilingus while the other provides manual masturbation.

Mutual masturbation involves fondling and caressing as well as manual manipulation of the clitoris. The success of each woman in achieving a full orgasm depends on her sensitivity and her partner's skill at this technique.

Tribadism is a rare activity among homosexually oriented women; it involves one partner mounting the other and bringing her to orgasm through body rubbing. As this is a face-to-face, heterosexual-like activity, its success depends largely on the psychological needs of the partners to act out a man-woman situation. (A *dildo*—an artifical phallus that is strapped on—may sometimes be used to achieve this effect.)

Multiple sex is also a rarity among homosexually oriented women. Occasionally, a "three way" happens; almost never are there more participants than that. The rarity of multiple sex among women is consonant with their emphasis on love and other tender feelings rather than on sex *per se.* Likewise, sado-masochistic *sexual* activities are uncommon among homosexually oriented women, although the masochistic need for emotional confrontation is not unusual (many of these women secretly enjoy domination, humiliation, or other psychic pain).

Women are generally less aroused by pictorial stimuli or other sensual-fantasy material than are men. This is certainly true of homosexually oriented women, who do not use nude photos or pornographic books for sexual arousal. (There is enjoyment of photos of attractive women from an aesthetic viewpoint, however.) Nor do homosexually oriented women use "poppers" to improve an orgasm, although many do use marijuana to increase tactile sensitivity.

Homosexually oriented women also frequent gay bars (some of which are exclusively for women, while others have a mixed homosexual clientele). These are, like gay bars for men, also for the dual purposes of socializing and finding pickups. A pickup in a gay bar for women is less casual than in a male gay bar: one woman may gaze at another for a long while (even for four or five successive nights) before she has courage enough to take the initiative and introduce herself. Also, her hopes are on the prospect of a long-term relationship with the other woman rather than on a "one-night stand." The other main way of meeting prospective lovers is through friends and acquaintances—by ordinary socializing. Street cruising among women is generally confined to eye contact. There are not acknowledged meeting places for homosexually oriented women on the order of turkish baths, parks, or beaches.

There is virtually no homosexual prostitution among women, although many prostitutes are thought to be homosexually oriented. That is, very rarely will one woman pay another to have sex with her. However, women who make their living through sexual encounters with men often prefer in their private lives to have an emotional and sexual relationship with a woman. (Many prostitutes pride themselves on not deriving pleasure from their sexual encounters with men.) Thus, although few homosexually oriented women become prostitutes, many prostitutes have homosexual inclinations.

As among homosexually oriented men, there is the necessity for secrecy and discretion in sexual activities among women. These women are careful about their image in the outside world and promote the illusion that they are heterosexually inclined by occasionally dating men with whom they work. Another expedient when two women are living together in a homosexual relationship is the maintenance of separate bedrooms in case parents or other outsiders should visit. Codes of honor and morality also apply to close relationships; betrayal of personal trust is very rare. Women seek out a long-term relationship with fairly reasonable expectations of the qualities in a lover that they are likely to find (their hopes and fantasies about prospective candidates are not so over-glorified as those of homosexually oriented men). They are prepared for monogamous relationships with absolute sexual fidelity, and these relationships generally last for several years. Again, the emphasis is on finding someone to end loneliness and someone to love, as well as someone to have sex with.

3

Causes of
Homosexual Orientation

Much of the psychological literature on homosexuality is concerned with etiology—the origins or causes of homosexual orientation in men and women. The question of psychological functioning is generally considered subordinate to the question of cause. Unfortunately, the psychological functioning of homosexually oriented individuals is often influenced by one etiological theory or another (for example, an individual may develop a very low self-concept because he considers his homosexual urges to be the product of mental disturbance). Therefore, before discussing psychological functioning we need to look at the major etiological theories currently in acceptance.

One of these theories is that homosexuality is a genetically transmitted "disease." This theory has been propounded by Kallmann (1952) in particular. Although the genetic theory has not been entirely discounted, there are many good arguments that seem to negate it. The foremost of these arguments is, of course, that if homosexuality is carried via a recessive gene, this trait should have died out long ago, assuming that homosexually oriented persons marry and reproduce with less frequency than heterosexually oriented persons. Also, most hereditary diseases have a rate of prevalence of 1 in 10,000; the ratio of individuals whose predominant sexual outlet is homosexuality to the rest of the population in the United States is at least 500 in 10,000.

Similarly, other hypothesized physiological differences have been negated. This is so with regard to endocrinal balance, chromosomes (or nuclear sex), and body build. With respect to endocrinal (or hormonal) balance, it has been established that hormones influence the individual's sex "drive" but not the *direction* of his sexual behavior. Homosexually oriented men when injected with androgen—the male sexual hormone—do not become sexually aroused by members of the opposite sex as a consequence; rather, they become more aroused by other men (Perloff, in Marmor, 1964). Likewise, when individuals who are predominantly homosexually oriented are compared with heterosexually oriented individuals on the basis of chromosomes or nuclear sex, no differences are found. (This determination is made by taking samples of bone marrow, blood, or skin tissue, all of which can be processed for a chromosomal count; Pare, in Marmor, 1964). Similar lack of differences are found in comparisons of body builds in homosexually oriented and heterosexually oriented individuals. Thus, at present, biological theories of homosexual etiology have been largely discounted in favor of psychological and sociological theories.

Probably the most widely held psychological theory on the etiology of homosexuality at the present time is Freudian. This theory is based on Freud's concept of the "identification" of the child with the parent of the opposite sex:

> In all cases examined we have ascertained that the later inverts go through in their childhood a phase of very intense but short-lived fixation on the woman (usually the mother) and after overcoming it they identify themselves with the woman and take themselves as the sexual object; that is, proceeding on a narcissistic basis, they look for young men resembling themselves in persons whom they wish to love as their mother loved them [Freud, 1930, page 10].

Extending and modifying this theory, most Freudians and particularly psychoanalysts believe that homosexuality is an illness to be treated and corrected. This, however, was not Freud's view. In his famous "Letter to an American Mother" (April 9, 1935), he wrote, "Homosexuality is assuredly no advantage, but is nothing to be ashamed of, no vice, no degradation, it cannot be classified as an illness; we consider it to be a variation of the sexual functions produced by a certain arrest of sexual development" (Freud, 1930, page 787). In other words, *different* psychological experiences in childhood do not necessarily imply subsequent psychological maladjustment in adulthood. Later, we shall see how most psychoanalytic thinkers reject this point of view.

Alfred Adler, a student of Freud's who subsequently parted ways with him, applied his concept of the "will to power" to homosexuality in women. He attributed the causes of homosexuality in women to "masculine protest"—women's reaction to being accorded an inferior social status; Freud attributed Lesbianism to "penis envy"— unconscious resentment stemming from the lack of a male sex organ. Both explanations are more valuable for suggesting possible reasons for masculine attributes in women than for explaining the basis of Lesbianism. Adler like Freud, did not equate homosexuality with psychological maladjustment but used "social interest" instead of sexual orientation as the criterion for the person's psychological health. That is, a person's commitment to the good of the society in which he lives was Adler's measure of that person's psychological well-being.

Post-Freudian psychoanalytic thinkers have modified the Freudian etiological theories of homosexuality. These analysts have based their theories on the patients they have seen in clinical practice and consequently have committed two fundamental errors in logic. The first is judging all people who regularly engage in homosexual behavior from the limited sample seen in the clinic or in private practice— that is, judging only from people who are unhappy enough or maladjusted enough to require psychotherapeutic aid. (Certainly no one would presume to describe the personalities of heterosexually oriented individuals from the ones seen in psychotherapeutic settings.) The second error in logic is in seeing most behavior as springing from neurotic or defensive motivations (for example, many Freudians believe positive achievement to be a sublimation of unacceptable sexual interests). With these cautions in mind, let us briefly examine some psychoanalytic theories of the etiology of homosexuality.

The belief that the cause of homosexuality is sexual immaturity is basic to most psychoanalytic thinking. Psychoanalysts maintain that individuals who regularly engage in homosexual behavior have not progressed through the various "psychosexual" stages to a culmination in heterosexual activities. This view is based on the Freudian concept of psychosexual development, which has been discarded or radically modified by most developmental researchers. Specifically, this theory holds that all persons begin their life with an experience of sensual pleasures focused on the oral zone (the region of the mouth and lips). Subsequently, sensuality is focused on the anal zone (typically, during the toilet-training period); as the individual approaches adolescence, the genital zone acquires prominence as the focus of sensual pleasures. The individual's experiences during each psychosexual stage determines his adult personality. For instance, psychoanalysts hypothesize that difficulties during the anal stage (perhaps as a result of severe toilet training) may stimulate the development of the "anal retentive" personality, who as a child took delight in saving or hoarding feces and as an adult is extremely neat, miserly, compulsive, or conscientious. Analysts, by similar conjecture, hold that persons who engage in homosexual behavior have been fixated at the oral or anal stages. This is based on the idea that persons who do not engage in heterosexual activities must be immature in their sexual development and consequently must have inadequately developed personalities as well. This definition is circular, it is largely conjecture, and it belies some ascertainable facts (for example, that many individuals who engage in homosexual behavior also participate in heterosexual activities, and that most persons who engage in homosexual relations are not demonstrably more immature than heterosexually oriented people). There are, of course, variations on this theory, but they almost always assume psychological immaturity or disturbance from the largely hypothetical psychoanalytic concepts. Included in these variations are the psychoanalytic thinkers who have written about homosexual behavior in women—analysts such as Helene Deutsch, Cornelia Wilbur, and May Romm. Deutsch, for example, wrote her famous article "Homosexuality in Women" (in Marmor, 1965) after analyzing only eleven cases. She attributed the homo-sexuality in these women to "penis envy" and disturbed mother-child relations; consequently, homosexuality in women was largely viewed as symptomatic of deeper prob-lems in personality functioning. Likewise, Wilbur (in Marmor, 1965) suggests several possible causes of female homosexu-ality: father "fixation," seduction in childhood (real or imagined) by an individual of the same sex, rape by a man, "penis envy," presence of a seductive father, renunciation of father at puberty as a response to felt rejection by him, prolonged absence of the mother, viewing the "primal scene," and sibling rivalry. She, too, expresses the pessimistic psychoanalytic viewpoint about psychological adjustment in women whose main interpersonal sexual outlet is homosexual relations.

Psychotherapist Albert Ellis sees homosexuality as based largely on fear of the opposite sex and feelings of inadequacy. He claims that since our society does condemn and punish individuals who engage in homosexual behavior, such behavior is "irrational" (inappropriate and dangerous) and consequently a manifestation of psychological disturb-ance. He even goes so far as to suggest that most individuals whose *exclusive* interpersonal sexual outlet is homosexuality are borderline psychotics just because of such "irrationality" (1965, page 82). This is both an irresponsible and an inappropriate contention. It is irresponsible because the diagnosis of "borderline psychotic" has a much more severe meaning for most psychiatrists and clinical psychologists than it has for Albert Ellis. (The term usually implies disordered thinking, inability to cope with interpersonal situations, faulty self-concept, and possible delusions or hallucinations.)

It is an inappropriate contention because it does not correspond to the research evidence we have on the relationship between homosexuality and psychological functioning. (Research studies are discussed in a later chapter.)

Donald Webster Cory (1951) gives a résumé of the possible causes of homosexual behavior among men in *The Homosexual in America*: the excessive love of a boy for his mother, eventuating in physical desire from which he later flees; a boy's attempt to replace his father as a result of the father's absence, death, or inadequacy, wherein all heterosexual love becomes equated with the love for his mother; a boy's identification with his mother and consequent attempt to be like her in every way; a boy's loss of his mother or lack of love from her, with the consequence that he seeks to play the role of wife and lover in the psychological relationship with the father; poor sex education, with sexual horrors vividly depicted and the boy being unable to link the thought of sex with his image of love between man and woman; the sanctification of woman as too pure to be dirtied by sex; withdrawal from competition with other males because of physical weakness or a predisposition to effeminacy; fear of competing with other men for a woman, resulting from an earlier aversion to competition with other boys on a physical basis; identification with girls because of inborn effeminate characteristics or those acquired as a result of previously mentioned causes; or the boy's introduction to positive homosexual experiences during adolescence. Many of these factors can be related to homosexuality among women, Cory maintains, if you add other causes as well, such as the search for power and domination, rebellion against the position of women in society, and the fear of pregnancy. Cory's most recent evaluation of the psychological health of individuals who regularly engage in homosexual relations is that these individuals are psychologically disturbed and should seek to change their sexual orientation. (Cory now holds a position almost identical to that of Albert Ellis, with whom he has collaborated on several books and articles.)

These etiological theories are not completely wrong or distorted. But they do imply an unyielding *psychic determination*: the idea that particular experiences in childhood necessarily create psychological maladjustment in later years. But in fact, youthful traumatic experiences as perceived in adulthood are usually seen in perspective and thus are softened; and distorted attitudes learned when young become modified by subsequent experiences. Because psychological functioning is determined through the complex interaction of intra-psychic, interpersonal, and environmental influences, identification of a disturbance in one of these areas does not mean that, on a global basis, the individual's psychological functioning will be damaged.

Several considerations about homosexuality must be mentioned here. First of all, many homosexual experiences emerge from situational opportunities such as college or military living arrangements. These experiences are based on the conjunction of diffuse sexual energy (or *pansexual* drive) and homosexual urges, both of which are common to all species, human and infrahuman (Ford and Beach, 1951). Paul Goodman (1960), in *Growing Up Absurd*, has pointed out how adults teach younger people to deny or reject their natural sexual urges when these urges are directed to members of their own sex. This is only one of the lies or hypocrisies we perpetrate on young people in our society, he asserts.

The social-learning point of view acknowledges a homosexual orientation or pattern of sexual preference. According to these theorists, a "homosexually oriented" individual is one whose interpersonal sexual experiences are predominantly with members of his own sex; this orientation originates in direct or indirect (symbolic) sexual experiences with members of the same sex. There must be positive attraction to, or experience with, members of one's own sex as a precondition for a homosexual orientation. Other factors may contribute to the development of a homosexual orientation, but the basis of the orientation is *the positive association with homosexual stimuli.* (Social-learning theory also holds that homosexuality is not a "second-best" form of sexuality compared with heterosexuality and is not necessarily coupled with fear of the opposite sex; many homosexually oriented persons also engage in, and enjoy, heterosexual relations.) Likewise, through the process of "cross-sex identification" a person may be more likely to turn to members of his own sex to satisfy sexual needs, but this is not a prerequisite for a homosexual orientation, nor is it probably applicable to most individuals who are homosexually oriented in general. Thus, a homosexual orientation is *multidetermined*, created by the conjunction of past experience and present circumstances. This social-learning approach to the etiology of homosexual behavior would hold that there is no *a priori* relationship between homosexuality and psychological disturbance. Inefficiency in coping with life's problems may be learned concomitantly with homosexual predispositions, but this does not happen invariably, nor is either one a *cause* of the other.

4

4

Psychological Adjustment
and Normality

It is entirely feasible to discuss the psychological concomitants of homosexuality without talking about etiology. As suggested above, different or even disturbed psychological experiences in childhood do not necessarily indicate personality disturbance in adulthood. Many theoreticians in the behavioral sciences have failed to consider this fact. Since the question of psychological adjustment of individuals who engage in homosexual behavior hinges on the criteria for such adjustment, this chapter discusses several different schemata for psychological adjustment, mental health, and normality, including some that are entirely compatible with a behavioral definition of homosexuality.

Daniel Offer and Melvin Sabshin (1966), in their book *Normality*, delineate four different perspectives of normality: normality as health, as utopia, as average, and as process. The first perspective, "normality as health," takes the traditional medical-psychiatric approach, which equates normality with health and sees health as an almost univeral phenomenon:

Many investigators have assumed behavior to be within normal limits when no manifest *35* pathology is present. Concentration is then focused upon definitions of pathology, leaving the large residue as "normal" or "healthy." Transposed upon a scale, normality would be the major portion of a continuum and abnormality would be the smaller remainder. This definition of normality seems to correlate with the activity of the model of the doctor who attempts to free his patients from grossly observable symptoms. To this physician, the lack of unfavorable symptoms indicates health. Health in this context refers to a *reasonable* rather than an *optimal* state of functioning. The psychiatrist subscribing to such an approach is interested in the prevention of disease; for him, prevention implies the treatment of the symptoms that overtly interfere with the adequate functioning of the patient [pages 99–100].

There are many difficulties inherent in defining normal behavior in terms of this medical perspective. Probably the major difficulty is based on semantic or linguistic confusion. That is, when we speak about deviant behavior as "sickness," we are using a *metaphor* rather than an isomorphic description. Illness is something with which every person, at one time or another, has had some experience. The concept of illness is therefore readily available to our minds when we want to characterize some acute difficulty or aberration. Thus, we hear of "social ills," "our sick society," a "mentally ill" person, and so on. This characterization is used by the most sophisticated writers and critics in our culture, as well as by the most unthinking hacks. The problem in using these medical metaphors for deviant behavior is that, aside from identifying a phenomenon as a source of difficulty, these terms ultimately *obscure* the issues. Let us take an example: in the last few years, many deviant behaviors have been identified as "sick" or as manifesting "mental illness." One of these is *gambling*. Gambling is not literally a disease, in the sense that it is the product of germs or viruses or bacteria. There is no *one* etiology, or causal agent, that produces the gambling behavior. The sequence of behavior is not the same for all gamblers, and there is no "prognosis" for this "sickness" as such. Whether gambling is communicable or not, like some diseases, is open to question. And whether we should try to "cure" gambling is a value judgment based on personal bias and individual background, rather than on an objective medical decision.

Also, the characterization of deviates from societal norms as disturbed or "ill" presents another problem. This is the danger of establishing a model of conformity, so that we label all who fail to conform as "sick, sick, sick" (Davidson, 1967). A further argument against the application of a medical model to psychosocial problems is given by Thomas Szasz (1960):

> The norm from which deviation is measured, whenever one speaks of a mental illness, is a *psychosocial* and *ethical* one. Yet the remedy is sought in terms of medical measures which—it is hoped and assumed—are free from wide differences of ethical value. The definition of the disorder and the terms in which its remedy is sought are therefore at serious odds with one another. The practical significance of the covert conflict between the alleged nature of the defect and the remedy can hardly be exaggerated.

As Szasz points out, to suppose that a psychiatrist or physician would be uninfluenced by his social and religious background in dealing with such "medical" problems as gambling, homosexuality, and marital infidelity is completely fatuous.

The concept of health and illness has been applied to homosexuality by many psychiatrists, psychologists, and social workers. The view of homosexuality as a "sickness" and of people who engage in homosexual behavior as "mentally ill" is manifestly inappropriate. Again, the term "sickness" as applied to homosexuality is used in a metaphoric rather than a literal sense. The implications of the "sickness" metaphor in relation to homosexuality are the following: all homosexuality has the same uniform etiology, or causal basis; homosexuality has a definite "prognosis";

homosexuality can and should be "cured"; and homosexual behavior is undesirable and to be avoided—like a communicable disease. It should be apparent that the "sickness" viewpoint is directly antithetical to the behavioral approach to homosexuality and has yet to be proved.

A variation of the "normality as health" definition has been stated by C. Daly King (1945) in his article "The Meaning of Normal." He defines normal as "that which functions in accordance with its design" (page 494). In view of the inherent *pansexual* nature of man and of the universality of homosexual behavior in the phylogenetic scale (Ford and Beach, 1951), it is not incorrect to view individuals who engage in homosexual behavior as normal according to King's criterion.

The next "functional perspective" of Offer and Sabshin is "normality as Utopia," which conceives of normality as a state of optimal personal functioning or self-actualization. This would make a rarity of the normal man, for at best only two or three per cent of the people in Western society are actualizing their potentials or are fully functioning. Such an extreme definition of normality and mental health is obviously not applicable as a *universal* criterion. Rather, self-actualization characterizes the psychological functioning of only a segment of the population. Discussions of self-actualization and positive mental health have tended to be very nebulous, especially in delineating the attributes of these phenomena. For example, in her book *Current Concepts of Positive Mental Health*, Marie Jahoda (1959) reviews the psychological literature on mental health and then presents six main criteria for positive mental health: attitudes toward the self; growth, development, and self-actualization; integration; autonomy; perception of reality; and environmental mastery.

The first criterion, "attitudes toward the self," includes several components. One is the availability of the self to consciousness; another, the reality and veracity of the self-concept. Also important here is the relation of the self-concept to the sense of identity, as well as the individual's acceptance of his own self as it presently exists.

"Growth, development, and self-actualization" is Jahoda's second criterion of positive mental health. Complementary to this is the degree to which the person utilizes his abilities. Also, the individual's orientation to the future is important—he should have a lively interest in the future, and not an obsessive anticipation that excludes present realities and pleasures. The person's investment in living must manifest itself in his on-going behavior.

The third criterion, "integration," entails the harmonious relationship of the psychic forces. The person must also have a unifying outlook on life, in that he has one overall frame of reference or "myth-system" to order the diverse data of his life. This "geist" will provide the individual with a resistance to stress as well.

"Autonomy," the fourth criterion, emphasizes independence, inner-direction, and self-reliance. The question here is whether the person will be able to decide with facility and dispatch what will be best for himself in relation to his own needs. (Perhaps the largest gap in interpersonal situations is that people are afraid or embarrassed to declare their own needs. This is exacerbated by the fact that people have a tendency to impose their own needs and expectations on others, thus depriving others of their autonomy.)

Jahoda's fifth criterion, "perception of reality," includes the absence of extreme need-distortion (as when an angry person sees everyone else as belligerent and hostile) and the ability to empathize with another person.

"Environmental mastery," the sixth criterion, encompasses several factors. One is the ability to love; as Erich Fromm has demonstrated in *The Art of Loving*, this would take several forms, not just husband-wife or parent-child love. Also included is efficacy in work and play, as well as adequacy in love and other interpersonal relationships. The person must be able to meet situational requirements, to adapt and adjust where necessary, and to cope with his problems effectively.

Jahoda believes these criteria to be operational in the sense that they can be proved empirically. However, many of the terms she uses, such as "integration," do not seem to have behavioral referents. Nevertheless, we can say that a person who closely approximates these six criteria would manifest superior psychological functioning.

Many psychologists—Goldstein, Bühler, Rogers, Maslow, Shostrom, and others—have tried to describe the qualities of the self-actualizing person. These theorists have included many of the attributes of positive mental health that Jahoda listed, as well as creativity, spontaneity, strong ethical principles, identification with mankind, and a good sense of humor. Again, there is the problem of specifying these qualities in objective behavioral terms. But their value in suggesting the attributes of superior psychological adjustment obtains nevertheless. It has been demonstrated, in recent research studies, that some individuals who engage in homosexual behavior very definitely meet these criteria for positive mental health and self-actualization.

Offer and Sabshin's third perspective of normality, after health and Utopia, is "normality as average," which essentially is based on the statistical principle of the bell-shaped curve as applied to physical, psychological, and sociological data. In contrast to the two perspectives described above, which visualize normality and abnormality as a straight-line continuum (they differ over where on the continuum the two are to be separated), the "normality as average" perspective sees the middle range as normal and *both* extremes as deviant. Offer and Sabshin argue, however, that this perspective often obscures the basis for a statement of abnormality or deviancy. That is, a number of behavioral scientists begin with the central values of the society, labeling them "normal," and then judge deviancy by its differentiation from the norms. This view, of course, omits all value judgments (which is where this perspective differs from the medical one). In the extreme, this makes a genius as deviant as an idiot, and a moral person as abnormal as a social psychopath.

Cohen (1959) has observed that deviant behavior can be the end result of two distinctly different processes. In one extreme form the "behavior is psychotic, neurotic, maladjusted, or otherwise pathological from a psychiatric point of view." Individuals who exhibit this type of behavior would be unable to cope effectively with life in virtually every society, and thus would be deviant in all of them. The other extreme is manifested by "clinically normal individuals" whose deviancy is due primarily to sociological factors. (This category might encompass everything from Quakers to social dropouts.) It is reasonable to suppose that many—if not most—individuals who engage in homosexual behavior fall into the latter definition of deviancy: discrepancy from society's professed values.

Another instance of the "normality as average" perspective is sex-researchers' operational definition of normality solely on a statistical basis. Along this line, Alfred Kinsey and associates (1948, 1953) have demonstrated that, on a statistical basis, homosexuality is very definitely not a rare and aberrant mode of sexual behavior but one occurring with considerable frequency in society. Their study demonstrated that at least 37 percent of the male population and a slightly lower percentage of the female population engages in homosexual activity between the onset of adolescence and old age. There is substantial evidence to suggest that the frequency of homosexual behavior would be even higher were it not for the repressive laws and social sanctions that society maintains.

The fourth perspective is "normality as process," which emphasizes that normal behavior is the end product of interacting systems that change over time. This view is held particularly by biologists and social scientists who subscribe to theories of biological and cultural evolution. Also under this heading can be considered theories of mental health that focus on life as *process* and on environmental mastery. One theory that fits this description well is Frederick Herzberg's "motivation-hygiene" theory, which yields a culture-fair definition of mental health and is the best framework for viewing psychological adjustment and positive mental health that I have encountered thus far. This theory grew out of a "critical incidents" study of job satisfaction among accountants and engineers in Pittsburgh industry (as reported in Herzberg and associates' *The Motivation to Work*, 1959). Subsequently, the theory was reaffirmed with a variety of different occupations and in several different countries. Essentially, motivation-hygiene theory began as a theory of job motivation that considered adjustment to work to be made up of two separate dimensions, the first component dealing with job satisfaction and the second with job dissatisfaction.

> The important feature of this theory is the implication that these two components of work adjustment are not opposites; rather, they are two distinct dimensions. The theory was generalized from data obtained by examining both the subjective and objective nature of jobs in which employees reported that they were unusually happy and unhappy [Herzberg and Hamlin, 1961, page 395].

Basically, the factors usually associated with happiness on the job were things that involved the *content* of the job, including achievement, task responsibility, professional advancement, interesting work, and recognition for achievement. On the other hand, the factors usually associated with job dissatisfaction were things that entailed the *context* in which the job was performed, such as poor company policies and administrative practices, poor supervision, poor interpersonal relationships (with superiors, peers, and subordinates), poor working conditions, and unfair salary schedules. Moreover, although the appearance of these latter factors could cause job dissatisfaction, their fulfillment alone could not stimulate happiness or job satisfaction. Rather, job satisfaction came only (for the majority of those employees interviewed) from "motivators"—achievement, responsibility, and so on. Thus, the two-continua notion of job satisfaction demonstrated that the opposite of job dissatisfaction is not job satisfaction but rather *no* job dissatisfaction, and the opposite of job satisfaction is not job dissatisfaction but *no* job satisfaction. Fulfillment of the "hygiene" factors, which deal with the job surroundings, would eliminate job unhappiness but would not of itself produce job satisfaction. The latter would grow only out of the availability of the "motivator" factors in the job. The transposition of motivation-hygiene theory to a concept of mental health has been done in an incisive fashion:

To generalize from job attitudes to mental attitudes, we can think of two types of adjustment for mental equilibrium. First, an adjustment to the environment, which is mainly an avoidance adjustment; second, an adjustment to oneself, which is dependent on the successful striving for psychological growth, self-actualization, self-realization, or most simply, being psychologically more than one has been in the past . . . The factors that determine mental illness are *not the obverse* of the mental health factors. Rather, the mental illness factors belong to the category of hygiene factors, which describe the environment of man and serve to cause illness when they are deficient but effect little positive increase in mental health. They are factors that cause avoidance behavior; yet, as will be explained, only in the "sick" individual is there an attempt to activate approach behavior [Herzberg, 1966, pages 78-79].

According to this schema, then, *normality* is defined in terms of the individual's acknowledgment (consciously, or tacitly by his behavior) of these two sets of needs and his desire to fulfill both sets of needs *given the opportunity*. For example, the jobless young man in the slums seeks both a meaningful job and better hygiene, such as good food and clothing, and thus is normal, according to this theory. Positive mental health would depend on availability and utilization of motivators and proper hygiene factors in the person's phenomenonological world.

We can examine sexual behavior in the light of this mental health paradigm. Tentatively, we can say that sexual behavior of any type is an attempt to satisfy a cyclical physiological need and consequently can be a source of only temporary satisfaction. That is, since any sexual act can bring only temporary pleasure and repletion of the physiological need, sex can never be a source of permanent happiness and fulfillment for the individual. Thus we can categorize sex along with eating, sleeping, and elimination as basic, cyclical needs that must regularly be attended to; these needs, when satisfied, can be a source of intense but only evanescent pleasure. In the framework of motivation-hygiene theory, emotional disturbance results when a person disregards the motivators and tries to derive permanent fulfillment and happiness from one or more of the hygiene factors. Examples of this would be the glutton who lives to eat rather than eats to live and the nymphomaniac who compulsively copulates. Thus, as long as sex (or any other hygiene factor) does not become an obsession, as long as it is recognized as being only a means of satisfying a bodily need and consequently a source of temporary pleasure, and as long as it is used in conjunction with—rather than to the exclusion of—the self-actualization factors, then the individual is psychologically healthy. By this account, the various types of homosexual behavior are legitimate means of satisfying the hygiene factors of sex, just as individual masturbation and the various kinds of heterosexual behavior all are.

According to this theory, then, life satisfactions should stem from motivation factors, and life dissatisfactions from hygiene factors. There has been some ambiguity about the role of interpersonal relations in the theory. "Interpersonal relations" is a hygiene factor and should not be a source of life satisfactions, with two exceptions. The first is when an individual's psychological functioning is improved as a result of his relationship with another person; the learning aspect of the relationship is, in essence, a motivator; the second is when the attainment of harmonious relationships is viewed as an achievement, as it could be to a marital counselor, a business manager, or a conscientious hostess. Thus, when a person perceives interpersonal relations to be a major source of satisfaction in life, the exact meaning of these relationships for him should be investigated.

One further caution is necessary. The application of motivation-hygiene theory to a concept of mental health is still tentative:

> Those factors found meaningful for industrial job satisfaction may not be complete or may not be sufficiently descriptive to encompass the total life picture of an individual . . . Other factors may

be necessary to describe the motivators in this larger sense. Whatever they may be, the criteria for their selection must include activity on the part of the individual—some tasks, episode, adventure, or activity in which the individual achieves a growth experience and without which the individual *will not* feel unhappy, dissatisfied, or uncomfortable [Herzberg, 1966, pages 81-82].

Herzberg suggests that "artistic and scholarly interest, receptive openness to new insights, and true relaxation and regrouping of growth potentials (as contracted with plain laziness) are all achievements or elements in achievement" (1966, page 82) and consequently come under the heading of motivators. This framework for viewing normality and mental health seems to be the most workable and sensible of all the schemas considered above. It suggests that normality is a widespread phenomenon, characterizing the vast majority of the population, and that positive mental health is potentially within reach of everyone, dependent on an individual's fulfillment of his unique potentialities.

5

Homosexuality
and Heterosexuality

This chapter serves to complete a frame of reference that will help you view the empirical research studies to be discussed in the next two chapters. Some of the nuances of homosexuality (and heterosexuality) are considered here.

Homosexuality: Differences Between Women and Men

Just as it would be fatuous to deny the real differences that exist between heterosexuality and homosexuality, or between men and women, so would it be fatuous to imagine that no differences exist in the consequences of homosexual behavior for the psychological functioning of women and of men. There are frequently different social-learning experiences in the backgrounds of women who engage in homosexual behavior from those in the backgrounds of the men who do.

Clara Thompson, in her well-known essay "Changing Concepts of Homosexuality in Psychoanalysis" (in Green, 1962), contended that women who engage in homosexual behavior are more likely to be better adjusted psychologically than men who do. She believed that this was due largely to society's contrasting attitudes and postures toward homosexual behaviors (and other behaviors suggesting *differentness*) among women and men.

For example, women are allowed "greater physical intimacy with each other without social disapproval" than is the situation for men. (Among women, embracing and kissing as forms of friendly expression are sanctioned. For men, there is a taboo on even a close friendship with one's own sex, which creates a climate of "compulsive heterosexuality" for men.)

Women are permitted to live together in complete intimacy without social disapproval or other sanctions in most communities. Such is not true for men; in similar arrangements, they often encounter harassment and marked hostility from members of the community.

Men are considered weak or disturbed when they choose a homosexual adjustment, since they generally have sufficient opportunity to meet and have sexual relations with members of the opposite sex. For them, homosexuality is regarded as a totally unacceptable substitution. The consequences of this attitude for the self-concept are illustrated in the case of Ron Russell below.

Ron Russell

Ron Russell is a 27-year-old instructor in French literature at a small California college. He was the younger of two children and had an Episcopalian upbringing. His father, who was considerably older than Ron's mother, seemed distant from him as he was growing up; Ron was more comfortable with his older sister and his mother than with his father. Despite this psychological distance, his father wanted Ron "to have the best": his parents sent him to preparatory school and furnished him with an extensive wardrobe at considerable financial sacrifice. Ron did his undergraduate studies at a large midwestern university; he spent his junior year in France, living with a family and attending the Sorbonne. He completed a master's thesis at another midwestern university on the symbolism of Proust; his doctoral dissertation, which is now near completion, is on the French surrealistic poets. As yet, he has not had to worry about serving in the military, because his draft board grants him an occupational deferment for his college teaching.

Ron first became aware of his homosexual impulses when he mistakenly wandered into a Parisian gay bar during his junior year abroad. He had several homosexual encounters that year and after he returned to America. These sexual activities expanded even more in graduate school, when he took on a lover (his sexual repertoire expanded from passive to active partnership in fellatio, active and passive partnership in anal intercourse, and other practices such as "around the world"). With this expansion of homosexual activity came a concomitant increase in feelings of guilt, shame, and self-disgust. Ron could not accept his homosexuality: he had been imbued too strongly with social attitudes against this orientation. Consequently, he engaged in a diversity of self-destructive behaviors, including over-indulgence in alcohol and tranquilizing drugs and sexual promiscuity. He was not candid about his life situation with his lover—concealing his other sexual affairs and the fact that he was in psychotherapy—and they parted; subsequently, his promiscuity increased greatly. (Ron has tried sex with a woman but did not particularly enjoy it.)

Ron is a short, good-looking young man: he resents people characterizing him as "cute," but the term does fit him. He is of bright-average intelligence but emotionally immature—his cognitive insights into his problems are not integrated at an emotional level. He is disgusted with his homosexual orientation but cannot curb his desires or see any real alternative. Psychotherapy only increased his anxiety without changing his behavior; in fact, he took to liquor and tranquilizers to curb the anxiety generated by the psychotherapeutic insights he gained. Like many homosexually oriented men, he does not know where he is going in life: one of his favorite songs is the theme from "The Valley of the Dolls," which asks, "Where am I going? What will I learn? Why?" It is likely that Ron will do well professionally but that he will remain in a personal quandary, unable to dissociate his sexual orientation from his negative self-concept.

On the other hand, since women generally have fewer opportunities to meet a wide range of potential sexual companions of the male sex, homosexuality is more excusable for them and is not necessarily viewed as a weakness or as a manifestation of psychological disturbance.

There are often factors that complement the arguments above. Women are very seldom arrested for engaging in homosexual behavior, whereas men are frequently arrested for involvement in situations surrounding homosexual encounters. There is less disparagement of and retribution against women who are mannish than against men who are effeminate, or "swish." Likewise, women who engage in homosexual relations are often much less readily identifiable by the lay public than their male counterparts.

Women in our society, whatever their choice of sexual outlets, are much more oriented to love relationships (of long duration) and less to the sexual factors alone than are men. Men are inculcated into the virtues of having many sexual partners and relationships. Thus, there is less "bed-hopping" and promiscuity among women than among men in our society, regardless of sexual orientation.

Also, women are generally more sensitive to others' emotional needs as well as to their own needs than are men. Sidney Jourard (1964), in *The Transparent Self*, maintains that this sensitivity is a characteristic of psychological well-being. He further holds that "self-disclosure" is more characteristic of women than men and that this has a consequent effect on both physical and psychological health:

If self-disclosure is an empirical index of "openness," of "real-self being," and if openness and real-self being are factors in health and wellness, then the research in self-disclosure seems to point to one of the potentially lethal aspects of the male role. Men keep to themselves, and impose thereby an added burden of stress beyond that imposed by the exigencies of everyday life [pages 47-48].

Cumulatively, all these factors suggest that women who engage in homosexual behavior are better adjusted psychologically than men who do. (The next chapter considers empirical research studies on the relationship between homosexuality and psychological functioning among both men and women.)

The Advantages of Homosexuality

The consequence of an individual's choosing homosexual outlets is not exclusively the inconvenience and frustration that results from all the societal pressures and laws against this form of sexuality. There are advantages as well.

First of all, sexual behavior, whatever form it takes, is generally pleasurable and stimulating. This certainly is as applicable to a homosexual experience as it is to a heterosexual one. In fact, homosexual experiences are generally characterized by attributes that are not so prevalent in heterosexual sex. Perhaps the major attribute is mutual concern and respect of the partners for each other. Related to this concern is the fact that when two people of the same sex are having sexual relations, they know, to a certain extent, what pleases the other (a man knows what feels good to a man, and a woman knows what feels good to a woman). This fact is especially true for women, because in heterosexual relations women are often merely used by their partners and gain little pleasure themselves, whereas in homosexual relations the partners are cognizant of what is required for the maximum pleasure of both.

Also, the social arrangements preparatory to a homosexual experience are much more direct and honest than in heterosexual situations. Generally before having sex with a woman, a man must wine and dine her, convince her that he is interested in her mind and personality, and (sometimes) that he loves her. With respect to homosexual situations (especially among men), there is more often an understanding that, at least initially, there is to be "sex for sex's sake." The prospective partners typically do not have to feign love or any other emotion that would be manifestly false at this point in the relationship. Sometimes these arrangements continue and result in a meaningful relationship; otherwise, the arrangement is merely a one-time sexual experience, valid and enjoyable in itself.

Another advantage of homosexuality is that the homosexually oriented individual, if he is reasonably uninhibited and self-accepting, will be able to find companionship wherever he goes in the world. Since there is such great pressure against the minority group to which he belongs, a sense of camaraderie has developed among homosexually oriented persons. Thus, wherever he travels, the homosexually oriented person is apt to discover other people of like sexual disposition who will introduce him to that place and its highlights.

A tangential benefit of choosing homosexual outlets to fulfill sexual and interpersonal needs is that the homosexually oriented individual is usually single and therefore will have a larger part of his income at his disposal for his own pleasure than if he is married. The same benefits would, of course, be available to any single person, regardless of sexual orientation. And many homosexually oriented persons *are* married, although the majority are not. (The financial benefits of being single are more available to men than to women, who have to support themselves on a woman's salary—generally inferior to a man's salary in our economy.)

All these advantages associated with homosexuality do not necessarily outweigh the problems resulting from the choice of a homosexual mode of adjustment (such as the fear of arrest, social ostracism, and blackmail), but these advantages certainly do make life more livable for the homosexually oriented individual.

The Disadvantages of Heterosexuality

When writers have discussed homosexuality, they have generally omitted a consideration of what is wrong with heterosexuality. They have implied, by this omission, that heterosexual relations are always idyllic, harmonious, or blissful. On the contrary, many prominent authors, including Erich Fromm, Albert Ellis, and Betty Friedan, have discussed the pathology that exists in a large percentage of heterosexual relationships in Western society. Fromm (1956), in *The Art of Loving*, has commented on the depersonalizing quality of life in an industrial society, where people evaluate themselves and other people as objects to be bought and sold in the personality market. He notes that this is particularly true in situations where people are seeking marriage partners. People are attuned to being loved rather than to giving love (and similarly more interested in receiving pleasure in sex than in giving pleasure). Fromm's evaluation seems especially pertinent to heterosexual relations, although it has some application to homosexual relations as well.

Albert Ellis has pointed out that people enter marital situations with unreasonable expectations about marriage. They often have irrational, romantic ideas about love and sex, which exclude a give-and-take quality from the relationship. (He notes that, despite society's prevalent attitudes about the desirability of marriage, this social institution is not appropriate for everyone.) The immaturity and irrationality of many people who enter the marital situation, in conjunction with the inherently stressful nature of the situation itself, account for the great number of divorces in Western society (and there would be still more divorces if it were not for the pressures of religious beliefs or of "keeping the family together" that maintain many bad marriages).

Betty Friedan (1963), in *The Feminine Mystique*, described the constricting situation that marriage is for most women in America. Women are often treated as chattel or the personal property of their husbands and are expected to be happy with just the mundane chores of housekeeping. They have not been encouraged to fulfill their unique potentialities but rather have been told to live through their husband's accomplishments.

Cumulatively, all these aspects of heterosexuality mean that there are problems inherent in heterosexual relations, just as there are problems intrinsic to homosexual relations (or to all human relations, for that matter). This discussion of heterosexuality is intended to be not an attack but rather the offering of new factors necessary to a comparison of psychological functioning between homosexually and heterosexually oriented individuals.

6

Psychological
Research Studies

At the present time, there seem to be two opposing trends in the behavioral sciences. One is that of emphasis on empirical research based on the scientific method; this cause is championed largely by experimental and (some) clinical psychologists. The other trend is the psychoanalytic one, a pseudoscientific approach that has depended on an amalgamation of mythical notions and manifestly poor research. This approach is taken mostly by psychiatrists and psychiatric social workers, who have arrived at a position where they seem to feel obligated to support the status quo in the behavioral sciences. Unfortunately, the opinion of the latter group concerning the psychological concomitants of homosexuality is the one held by most behavioral scientists and laymen as well, despite research findings that support a different point of view. Research on psychological aspects of homosexuality obviously holds more than just an academic interest, for it may determine the consequent actions taken in the future toward individuals who engage in homosexual activities. Lionel Trilling, in a review of the first Kinsey report (in Geddes, 1954), commented on a new power of the social sciences: the social sciences no longer just describe what people do, they have the ability to "manipulate and

adjust." Thus, according to Trilling, the act of comprehension becomes "an act of control." If this thesis is correct,
then social actions should be based on good empirical
research rather than on pseudoscientific, armchair theorizing.

At this point, it is appropriate to review the
empirical research studies that have been done on the
psychological adjustment of individuals who engage in
homosexual behavior. In the context of most of these
studies, "psychological adjustment" can be defined as the
possession of those values, emotions, and perceptions that are
necessary for successful living in society. ("Values" here can
be equated with the general and organized conceptions that
influence behavior.)

Prior to the last ten years, the psychological
research on homosexuality was limited and of dubious value.
One trend in this "early" research stemmed from cases seen
in the clinic and in private-practice psychotherapy. The
researchers generalized from limited and distorted samples of
individuals who engage in homosexual behavior, and in some
cases they made generalizations about homosexuality from
the study of one or two clients. Also, these studies often had
a psychoanalytic framework, and the findings fitted in a
Procrustean fashion to psychoanalytic concepts such as
"unresolved Oedipus complex" and "penis envy." Other
studies on homosexuality—particularly those done by clinical
psychologists—have concentrated on finding psychometric
signs to identify homosexual components of an individual's
personality. These studies have usually been founded on the *a
priori* assumption that individuals who engage in homosexual
behavior are emotionally disturbed and that homosexual
behavior itself is something undesirable in a person's behavioral repertoire. Joseph Deluca (1966) states:

> Difficulties have also arisen from the fact that
> many Es [experimenters] assume by definition
> that homosexuality is pathologic, a view which
> often resulted in a refusal to look for psycho-
> pathology in a comparative sense [page 205].

Such psychometric signs seem to point to the
deviant characteristic of the homosexually oriented person

(just as a social dropout or an independently thinking scientist would be identified as deviant) rather than to his homosexuality *per se*. (Mensh, 1965). Desmond Curran and Denis Parr (1957)—one a British consulting psychiatrist, the other a research fellow—made a careful study of one hundred cases that had been seen in psychiatric practice. They concluded that the "homosexuals" they studied were "on the whole successful and valuable members of society, quite unlike the popular conception of such persons as vicious criminals, effete or depraved" (page 19). They found only about 20 per cent "obviously pansy," and saw no reason to regard most of the persons as immature—physically, intellectually, or emotionally. "Only half of the patients showed significant psychiatric abnormality other than their sexual deviation, and such associated abnormalities were often slight. Moreover, many of these abnormalities were explicable as a reaction to the difficulties of being a homosexual" (page 19). Remember that these generally positive conclusions are based on people who are seeking psychological treatment—suggesting that the majority of homosexually oriented individuals who do not feel impelled to seek psychotherapeutic aid may be even better functioning in general than those who do.

Isador Rubin (1961) reports that an anonymous "homosexual" physician, writing in one of the leading British medical publications, cited sixteen case histories of persons known to him in support of the same thesis. The majority of these individuals, he asserted, were well-adjusted and respected members of their community. There are those who would discount the value of this report because the physician was homosexually oriented (by his own admission) and therefore biased. It is important to remember that the topic of homosexuality is an emotionally charged one and that it is virtually impossible to be cool, objective, and dispassionate about it.

A survey of a group of one hundred South African "homosexuals" (fifty males and fifty females) and a control group of "heterosexuals" was described in the *British Medical Journal* by Renee Liddicoat (1957). None of the individuals studied was seeking psychiatric help, and none of them had been charged with illegal homosexual activities. One of

Liddicoat's major findings was that the "homosexual" group did not reveal any evidence of trends toward a psychopathic personality. A few individual subjects gave evidence of being highly neurotic, but such signs were discovered among members of the control ("heterosexual") group also.

Similarly, Michael Schofield (1966), in his book *Sociological Aspects of Homosexuality*, reported like findings with a sample of 300 British subjects. Each subject was interviewed and then asked to complete a verbal reasoning test and a personality inventory. During the interview, the research worker sought factual information on family background, social behavior, and sexual activities. Comparisons were made between six groups: inmates of prisons convicted of homosexual offenses with adults; inmates of prisons convicted of sexual offenses with boys under sixteen; "homosexuals" who were under psychiatric treatment in a hospital or outpatient clinic; "non-homosexuals" who were under psychiatric treatment in a hospital or outpatient clinic; "homosexuals" who had not received psychiatric treatment and who had not been convicted for homosexual offenses; and "non-homosexuals" who had not received psychiatric treatment and who had not been convicted for sexual offenses. Schofield expected his research to show large differences between each homosexual group and its matching control: in actuality, there were small differences between the pairs of matched groups and large differences between the homosexual groups. Thus, the psychological functioning of the homosexual and heterosexual groups that had experienced neither psychiatric attention nor imprisonment was very similar, and was positive and productive as well.

One of the first (and most solid) studies in America of the psychological concomitants of homosexuality was that of Evelyn Hooker (1957) in "The Adjustment of the Male Overt Homosexual." In this study, there were thirty subjects each in the "homosexual" group and the "heterosexual" group, matched by pairs for age, education, and I. Q. In addition to the Otis Self-Administering Test of Mental Ability to determine intellectual level, the subjects were given the Rorschach Ink-Blot Test, the Thematic Apperception Test, and the Make-a-Picture-Story Test. All of these projective tests depend on the subject's needs influencing his imaginative productions: giving associations to the ink-blots on the Rorschach, making up stories in reaction to ambiguous drawings on the Thematic Apperception Test, and creating vignettes from a variety of common stimuli (such as house, dog, mother-figure) on the Make-a-Picture-Story Test. These tests were analyzed by expert clinical psychologists, who rated each subject on a five-point scale of personality adjustment without knowing the subject's sexual orientation from their "blind" analysis of the test protocols. The results indicated that the judges could not identify the sexual orientation of the subjects at better than a chance level, and that the ratings of the experimental group were not significantly different from those of the control group (that is, the "homosexual" subjects were rated as being no more disturbed than "heterosexual" subjects). In fact, there were no significant differences between the number of "homosexuals" and "heterosexuals" having a rating of 3 ("normal") or better for each judge; two-thirds of each group were assigned an adjustment rating of 3 or better. The experimental subjects were obtained through the Mattachine Society, however, and may not constitute a representative sample of individuals who engage in homosexual behavior. Hooker commented on this possibility: "No one knows what a random sample of the homosexual population would be like; and even if one knows, it would be extremely difficult, if not impossible, to obtain one" (1957, page 19). She drew the following tentative conclusions from her study: homosexuality as a clinical entity does not exist—its forms are as varied as those of heterosexuality; homosexuality may be a deviation in sexual pattern that is within the normal range, psychologically; and the role of particular forms of sexual desire and expression in personality structure may be less important than has frequently been assumed.

A similar study was reported by Doidge and Holzman (1960) in "Implications of Homosexuality Among Air Force Trainees." A battery of ten psychological tests, including two original tests, was administered to 80 enlisted airmen divided equally into four groups. Subjects were assigned to groups according to whether they were "heterosexual," "partly homosexual," or "markedly homosexual" in their psychosexual orientations.

> Only the markedly homosexual group gave test records that were strikingly different from the control groups, suggesting that markedly homosexual individuals are likely to be suffering from an emotional disorder which is relatively pervasive, severe, and disqualifying for military service. The partly homosexual group (composed of individuals who were predominantly heterosexual but with varying degrees of homosexual experience) gave test results that closely approximated the results of the two control groups. [Page 12].

These results may be accounted for, in part, by the fact that the "markedly homosexual" group (who had been arrested for sexual offenses while in the Air Force) evinced psychological disturbance or irrational behavior just by enlisting in the Air Force with full cognizance of their sexual orientation and the possible risks this would entail. However, the study nevertheless demonstrated that there is no *a priori* connection between homosexual behavior and personality disturbance, and that individuals who engage in homosexual activities are not necessarily psychologically maladjusted.

A study by Chang and Block (1960) was concerned with a test of the Freudian notion that homosexuality in the male is based on an over-identification with the mother figure together with an under-identification with the father figure. Two groups of subjects, equivalent in age, education, and socio-economic level, were used: a group of twenty males engaging, apparently successfully, in homosexual practices, and a group of "non-homosexual" males. Each subject described his ideal self, his mother, his father, and himself, by the use of a list of adjectives. On the basis of an "ego ideal" conception of identification, various identification scores and self-acceptance scores were obtained for each subject by comparing his description of his ideal self with that of the other individuals he described. The results indicated that the homosexually oriented males identified more with their mothers and less with their fathers than the heterosexually oriented males with whom they were compared. However, on the dimensions of self-acceptance and of the kind of "ego ideal" to which they aspired, the two groups of subjects did not differ significantly. This substantiates the idea that differences in social-learning history (etiological factors) do not necessarily mean differences in subsequent psychological adjustment.

Cattell and Morony (1962), studying seventy-eight incarcerated Australian "homosexuals" convicted of homosexual offenses, obtained test results that differed significantly from those of "normals." On their 16PF (Personality Factors) test, the "homosexuals" were similar to anxiety neurotics, similarity being indicated by a high-pattern similarity coefficient. In an attempt to rule out selection and incarceration effects, they compared their "convicted homosexuals" with a group of thirty-three "homosexuals not under arrest" and found the two group profiles very similar in shape and elevation. This is one of the few studies that has found definite differences in personality adjustment between individuals who regularly engage in homosexual behavior and those whose interpersonal sexual outlet is heterosexuality; there is a distinct possibility that these results are attributable to differences in cultural attitudes toward homosexuality. The conclusion of Cattell and Morony that "convicted and unconvicted homosexuals are *essentially* the same species" is exactly opposite to the findings of Schofield, described above.

Also using a prison population, Miller (1966) found, on the basis of personality tests, that there was no significant difference in rated psychological adjustment between incarcerated women who engage in homosexual activities in prison and those who did not.

Using an experimental group of forty college-educated "overt male homosexuals" and a matched "heterosexual" control group, Dean and Richardson (1964) found that, on the Minnesota Multiphasic Personality Inventory (a long questionnaire directed to psychological disturbance), "the profiles of the two groups were very similar with regard to both their shape and general elevation" (page 458). In addition, the "homosexual" profile fell within what has been defined as the "normal" range (below a T score of 70) as well as being only slightly elevated above that of the comparison group. The experimenters concluded that their results indicated that homosexually oriented subjects who are intelligent and functioning effectively do not manifest disturbance on the MMPI.

Joseph Deluca (1966) administered the Rorschach to twenty-five men who were being discharged from the armed services because of homosexual behavior and to a control group of twenty-five men who were temporarily confined to an Army hospital for upper respiratory infections (mostly bad colds). He concluded from his study that "homosexuals" do not constitute a homogeneous group and that homosexuality does not exist as a distinct clinical entity.

> The homosexuals varied from each other as much as they did from the normals in regard to the structure of their personality. They were also distinctly different from each other in the total number of purported signs of homosexuality they accumulated. Although not associated with the particular variation the symptoms took, the homosexuals evidenced large variation in the nature of their anxiety they were defending against. The psychoanalytic theories of homosexuality are not supported by the wide variation between subgroups. Previous studies have treated homosexuals as a homogeneous group. When Es [experimenters] assume that a non-homogeneous group is homogeneous there are bound to be discrepancies in the literature.
>
> The issue of whether homosexuals are more pathologic than normals, in the light of the present findings, seems to have been an unwarranted assumption, based more upon armchair theorizing than experimental evidence [page 206].

Marcel T. Saghir and others (1970*a*) conducted a controlled psychiatric study on the prevalence of psychopathology among a group of thirty-five unmarried men. They found slightly more disability and more clinically significant change in the lives of the homosexual men. They concluded that, "despite the slight increase in disability and the changes in their lives, the homosexual men functioned well" (page 1086).

With the exception of the Liddicoat and Miller studies, all the studies cited have used *men* who engage in homosexual activities as experimental subjects. There is a dearth of studies using *women* who engage in homosexual activities as experimental subjects. A search of the literature revealed only four such studies, one of which (Fromm and Elonen, 1951) was a study of one case, dealing with the projective test analysis of a woman whose predominant interpersonal sexual outlet was homosexual. The problems of generalizing from one case—which the authors of this study attempted to do—are obvious. Thus, we are left with the other studies. "Some Personality Variables in Overt Female Homosexuality" by Virginia Armon (1960) is a detailed study with a larger sample. Her experimental group consisted of thirty "overt female homosexuals" provided through the Research Committees of the Mattachine Society and One, Inc. All of the "homosexual" women in this study were committed to a life pattern of overt homosexual practice, all were making at least a "marginal adjustment" to the community aside from their homosexuality, and none was receiving psychotherapy or seeking help for personal problems. The "heterosexual" group was drawn from groups of mothers whose children participated in a pre-school program, and they met similar criteria to the experimental group. The intent of the study was not paired-matching but general comparability of the two groups for age, education, acculturation, and socio-economic status. One examiner individually administered the Rorschach and Figure Drawing Test to each subject. This examiner codified and mixed the raw test data before they were submitted to judges for ratings. Rorschach and Figure Drawing materials were judged independently. None of the judges was able to distinguish "homosexual" Rorschach records or Figure Drawings significantly better than chance; Armon concluded from this that homosexually oriented women cannot be distinguished from heterosexually oriented women on the basis of projective test performance. Armon further expanded on her results:

> The failure to find many clear-cut differences which are consistent for the majority of the group would suggest that homosexuality is not a clinical entity. On the basis of present indications it would seem unwise to make generalizations about female homosexuals as a group or to assume that homosexuality is necessarily associated with gross personality disturbance. The general absence of dramatic differences between the performance of the homosexuals and heterosexuals on projective tests should influence the conception of homosexuality as necessarily associated with deep repression and concordant limitations in personality functioning. In different areas a tendency to more seriously disturbed response was noted in the homosexual group, but would occur in only a few cases, usually less than one-third of the group. The impression is that the homosexual group, selected originally as making an adequate adjustment in society aside from their homosexuality, nevertheless contained a few more individuals who give deviant and disturbed responses in projective tests than were found in the heterosexual group. One could not describe the majority of the homosexual women as more poorly adjusted on the basis of their projective test performance. (1961, 308)

Essentially, then, Armon's results were the same as those found in most of the studies using men as experimental subjects.

June Hopkins (1969) measured twenty-four "Lesbians" and twenty-four "matched controls" with the 16PF personality inventory. She concluded that in place of the designation "neurotic" the following terms were preferable in describing the homosexually oriented woman: more independent, resilient, reserved, dominant, bohemian, self-sufficient, and more composed.

Marcel Saghir and his colleagues (1970b) also conducted a controlled psychiatric study on homosexually oriented women. The subjects were fifty-seven "homosexual" women and forty-three single "heterosexual controls." There were slightly more clinically significant changes and disability in the lives of the "homosexual" women as compared with the "heterosexual" women. The chief differences were in the increased prevalence of alcoholism and of attempted suicide. Despite these difficulties, they concluded, the homosexually oriented women were able to achieve, adapt, and be productive citizens.

The implications of these empirical psychological studies are inescapable. Homosexuality is not a clinical entity. Clara Thompson (in Green, 1962) has suggested that even as a symptom, homosexuality does not present a uniform appearance. She maintains that there are at least as many different types of homosexual behavior as heterosexual, and the interpersonal relations of "homosexuals" present the same problems found in heterosexual situations. Moreover, homosexual behavior is not necessarily an indication of personality disturbance, nor are individuals who engage in homosexual practices more apt to be psychologically maladjusted on the average than people who have a heterosexual orientation.

> . . . From the point of view of personal adjustment, it is highly questionable whether any sexual behavior exercised between consenting adults is of any real social importance. From a psychiatric point of view, the thing that counts seems to be the efficiency with which an individual functions in life—his usefulness, his enjoyment, and the success of his human interactions. If society has an interest here, it is certainly in the maintenance of high personal efficiency and low neurotic effects. In terms of this ideal, the particular sexual responses of individuals hardly seem to be of any major concern [Tripp, 1965, page 23].

The same view has been voiced by the highly respected Wolfenden Committee on homosexuality: "Homosexuality cannot legitimately be regarded as a disease," their 1957 report asserted, "because in many cases it is the only symptom and is compatible with full mental health in all respects."

7

A Personal
Research Study

Psychological research studies are always difficult to conduct when social behavior is being examined, and studies on sexuality are particularly difficult because of the defenses people build up in their attitudes toward sex. It may be helpful to look at the mechanics and results of a particular study I conducted in 1967 to see the limitations that a researcher must accept to achieve adequate scientific control. Despite these difficulties and limitations, the results were surprising.

The intent of my study was to determine empirically the relationship between homosexuality and psychological adjustment among women, using a relatively large sample. I strove to find about 150 subjects, with at least 75 to 100 of these homosexually oriented. I chose standard personality inventories primarily because the efficacy of these inventories in the assessment of human behavior has been repeatedly demonstrated since they were first systematically developed during World War I. The approach taken here was a group perspective as opposed to an individualized one. That is, standardized tests such as the personality inventory purposely do not tell very much about the individual as an individual; rather, they show how nearly he approximates a normal performance of "culturally prescribed tasks" (such as efficacy of interpersonal relationships and handling of stress). In the case of this study, the responses of the subjects to questions about their feelings and behavior yielded information about their relative psychological adjustment as compared with persons who had originally taken these tests. And, more specifically, there was an attempt to assess the psychological health of women who have made different sexual adjustments; that is, I wanted to compare the functioning of women who have chosen homosexual outlets as a means of fulfilling their sexual and interpersonal needs with those who have chosen heterosexual outlets. When I conceived the study, I intended to get a detailed sexual history from each subject. Unfortunately, this had to be omitted, because it would have aroused the suspicions of my heterosexually oriented subjects, who ostensibly were participating in research on "the mental health of women." I did not inform them that they were a "control" group to a group of homosexually oriented females, since this would have distorted their responses to the questionnaires. (It is a basic dictum of psychological research that you do not tell the members of a control group that they are there chiefly for comparison and not of interest by themselves in your research!)

The Important Questions

Given the condemnatory attitude of society toward homosexuality, there inevitably will be differences in the coping mechanisms, the values, and the personal experiences of women whose mode of satisfying their sexual needs is homosexual from those of women whose mode is heterosexual and who consequently do not have to contend with this societal pressure. This study was an investigation of these differences in four areas: psychological adjustment, effects of social acceptance, sex-role identification, and interpersonal relations. I hypothesized questions in each of these areas, as discussed below.

Although there are undoubtedly different social-learning experiences and personality traits that determine the mode of sexuality chosen, most research studies suggest that individuals who fulfill their sexual and interpersonal needs with members of their own sex appear to be as well adjusted psychologically as individuals who satisfy these needs with members of the opposite sex. The study sought to add more information to the data already gathered on this general question. Specifically, it investigated the question of neuroticism, which has been of particular interest in studies of the psychological concomitants of homosexuality. According to a social-learning theory of the acquisition of different types of sexual behavior, and also according to empirical psychological research, neuroticism—in the sense of general emotional overresponsivity—is no more likely to be characteristic of homosexually oriented individuals than of heterosexually oriented ones. However, there may be more variability in the patterns of psychological functioning among homosexually oriented people. This was one of the questions posed by the study.

Another was the effects of minority-group status on the members of the group. Individuals who engage in homosexual relations have been considered by some sociologists (Cory, 1963) to be part of a unique, largely invisible (but nonetheless real) minority group in society. These individuals are the object of negative, punitive, and prejudicial attitudes held by a large number of people. It is well known in the psychology of prejudice that individuals at whom constant censure is directed develop certain coping devices and self-perceptions in response to this prejudice. Drawing a parallel between discriminated-against groups (such as blacks and Jews) whose responses to prejudice have been studied and individuals who engage in homosexual relations (who are also the object of prejudice and scorn), I hypothesized that there would be greater independence and inner-direction in individuals who engage in homosexual relations than those who engage in heterosexual relations. However, there should be lower self-acceptance in the former group than in the latter.

Psychological research studies on personality characteristics of homosexually oriented individuals have suggested the importance of patterns of sex-role identification in the personalities of these individuals. That is, the behaviors and values of such individuals are often derived from the parent of the opposite sex; these individuals thus sometimes exhibit traits, behaviors, and values more characteristic of members of the opposite sex than members of their own sex. Such differences in sex-role identification are not necessarily related to psychological disturbance. However, it would be expected by this account that women who engage in homosexual relations will manifest more masculine behaviors and values than women who engage in heterosexual relations. So two other hypotheses of the study were that homosexually oriented women should be more like men in the acceptance or the owning of their aggressive feelings (which are a natural part of being human) than are heterosexually oriented women, and that homosexually oriented women should show more masculine motivational patterns with regard to work satisfaction than should heterosexually oriented women.

Another hypothesis was that there would be no differences between homosexually and heterosexually oriented women in the capacity for intimate contact—a reflection of the ability to have warm interpersonal relationships. This hypothesis was based on the idea that intimate contact is contingent on the *relationship* between two persons, regardless of gender. Also, for both groups of women, interpersonal relations should be more important than sex as a source of life satisfaction; this is consonant with the differences between the male and female orientation to sexual relations, women being more concerned about love relationships than with sexual gratification *per se*. Finally, in both groups, I expected that interpersonal relations should be as much a source of happiness as of unhappiness in life.

The Subjects of the Study

I tested the foregoing hypotheses by selecting two groups of subjects, one group whose principal interpersonal sexual outlet is homosexual and another group whose principal interpersonal sexual outlet is heterosexual. I had each subject complete a battery of psychological tests and personal data sheets and then compared the two groups of subjects in their responses to the test battery.

The eighty-one members of the experimental group—women whose principal interpersonal sexual outlet is homosexual relations—were affiliated with the Daughters of Bilitis, a women's organization that has a chapter in several large American cities (New York, Los Angeles, Philadelphia, San Francisco). The purpose of this organization, as described in its monthly magazine *The Ladder*, is "promoting the integration of the homosexual into society" by:

1. Education of the variant, with particular emphasis on the psychological, physiological, and sociological aspects, to enable her to understand herself and make her adjustment to society in all its social, civic, and economic implications. . . .

2. Education of the public at large through acceptance first of the individual, leading to an eventual breakdown of erroneous taboos and prejudices; through public discussion meetings; through dissemination of educational literature on the homosexual theme.

3. Participation in research projects by duly authorized and responsible psychologists, sociologists and other such experts directed towards further knowledge of the homosexual.

4. Investigation of the penal code as it pertains to the homosexual, proposal of changes to provide an equitable handling of cases involving this minority group, and promotion of these changes through due process of laws in the state legislature.

The Daughters of Bilitis takes its name from a poem in which Bilitis was a woman who befriended Sappho, the Lesbian poet. The two main foci of the organization are the publication of their magazine *The Ladder* and their weekly meetings. *The Ladder* is composed of essays on various aspects of homosexuality as well as short stories, poetry, book reviews, news items, and letters related to the place of the homosexually oriented individual in society. The weekly meetings include the general business of the organization, lectures by psychologists and other professional persons about homosexuality and effective functioning, and just plain socializing by the members of the D.O.B. When I addressed the New York chapter of the D.O.B. before asking their participation in my research, I was particularly impressed with the members' keen interest in theoretical and practical aspects of psychological functioning as well as with their lack of bitterness toward the greater society that had posed many problems for them. (Interestingly, only about one fourth of the members fitted the stereotype of "the Lesbian" in their physical appearance, voice, or gestures; the majority were not identifiable in regard to their sexual orientation.)

The sixty-seven members of the control group—women whose principal interpersonal sexual outlet is heterosexual relations—were affiliated with the women's volunteer division of an international service organization. Along with its main service function, this division seeks to promote *responsibility* for women in society (there is apparently no women's group directly comparable to the D.O.B. in furthering the integration of "heterosexuals" in American society.) There is the possibility that the members of the control group do not constitute a representative sample of American women. However, although these subjects may not have psychological adjustment representative of all women in the United States, the comparability of their group (with regard to promoting responsibility for women) to the D.O.B. is more pertinent to the present study than their "representativeness." (It is a point well taken that no one really knows about the psychological functioning of women in any developed society.)

Group identification was used as the criterion of present interpersonal sexual outlet. That is, in this study, affiliation with the D.O.B. was equated with a homosexual mode of adjustment, and affiliation with the women's volunteer division of the national service organization was equated with a heterosexual mode of adjustment. There is a possibility that this categorization through group-identification may have produced one or two errors, but the possibility is very slight.

The members of the experimental group probably do not constitute a representative sample of women who engage in homosexual relations, but no one knows what the demography and psychological functioning of this population are. There have been suggestions that the women who join the D.O.B. are better adjusted than the whole range of women who engage in homosexual relations, in general (Cory, 1965; Stearn, 1964). In order not to bias the study, therefore, the organization-joining trait of the members of the D.O.B. was controlled for with a comparable group of women (who have joined an organization which tries to further responsibility for women in American society). Hopefully, this eliminated one possible flaw of the study — that of obtaining the experimental group from an unrepresentative and better-than-average adjustment sample.

The characteristics of the two groups are listed below:

· All members of both groups were white.

· The members of the control group were significantly older than the members of the experimental group. In the control group, 82 per cent were 46 years or older, whereas 89 per cent of the experimental group were 45 years or younger.

· There were no significant differences found between the two groups with regard to educational background. The majority in both groups were high-school graduates with some college experience.

· A significantly greater proportion of the experimental group than of the control group had had psychotherapy (38 per cent as opposed to 3 per cent), although the majority of the subjects in each group had not had psychotherapy.

· A significantly greater proportion of the experimental group professed no religion (48 per cent, as opposed to 5 per cent among members of the control group). This is consonant with the fact that most formal religions do not accept individuals who engage in homosexual relations as worthy of membership in a congregation.

· The majority of the experimental group was holding salaried positions (89 per cent), whereas the majority of the control group did not work for a living (82 per cent).

· A large majority of the experimental group had never been married (77 per cent), while the majority of the control group were married at the time the study was done or had been married (89 per cent). Of those who had been married at one time in their lives, a significantly greater proportion of the experimental group had been divorced than had the control group (18 per cent as opposed to 4 per cent).

· All of the subjects were living in urban areas; the members of the experimental group were living in the New York, San Francisco, and Los Angeles metropolitan areas; the members of the control group, in the Cleveland metropolitan area.

The Test Battery

The test battery consisted of two personal data sheets and two personality inventories, and required slightly longer than one hour to complete. The first personal data sheet consisted of questions about demographic characteristics and produced the data described above. The second personal data sheet asked questions based on a motivational theory of job satisfaction and mental health. These questions dealt with the factors a person looks for in a job or task and the sources of happiness and unhappiness on the job and in life as well.

One of the personality inventories used was the Personal Orientation Inventory, a 150-item questionnaire designed specifically to measure the components of "self-actualization." The test yields a profile that includes twelve scales measuring time competency, inner-directedness, self-actualizing values, existentiality, feeling reactivity, spontaneity, self-regard, self-acceptance, view of the nature of man, synergy, acceptance of aggression, and the capacity for intimate contact. "Time competency" assesses the extent to which the person is oriented to the present, as opposed to being obsessed with his past or anticipating the future.

"Inner-direction" is a reflection of the degree to which the person's values and behaviors are his own—that is, whether he is guided more by internal motivations than by external influences. "Self-actualizing values" measures the degree to which the person holds and lives by values of self-actualizing people. "Existentiality" measures the ability to live without rigid adherence to dogmatic principles. "Feeling reactivity" measures sensitivity of responsiveness to one's own needs and feelings. "Spontaneity" evaluates the person's freedom to react spontaneously or to be himself. "Self-regard" measures affirmation of one's self because of one's strength as a person. "Self-acceptance" measures acceptance of one's self despite weaknesses or deficiencies; it is more difficult to achieve self-acceptance than self-regard. "View of the nature of man" measures the extent to which one sees man as essentially good and to which one can resolve the goodness-evil, masculine-feminine, selfishness-unselfishness, and spirituality-sensuality dichotomies in the nature of man. "Synergy" measures the ability to see opposites of life (such as work and play) as meaningfully related. "Acceptance of aggression" measures one's ability to accept one's natural aggressiveness as opposed to defensiveness, denial, and repression of aggression. And "capacity for intimate contact" measures one's ability to develop meaningful relationships with other human beings, unencumbered by exaggerated expectations and obligations (Shostrom, 1963).

The Personal Orientation Inventory, although recently developed, has norms for various adult groups—including, of course, those from a group of persons judged to be "self-actualizing" (functioning extremely well) by psychologists and psychotherapists. It was developed by Everett Shostrom, based on the theories of positive mental health and self-actualization of Abraham Maslow, Frederick Perls, Rollo May, David Reisman, and Albert Ellis. The P.O.I. manual illustrates sample profiles of self-actualizing persons, of persons of average adjustment, and of disturbed (hospitalized) individuals. This personality test is appropriate because it was designed to measure positive mental health as well as psychopathology. It was combined with a second personality inventory (a test specifically directed toward measuring neuroticism and emotional instability) to give an overall rating of psychological adjustment for each subject.

The second inventory was the Eysenck Personality Inventory, a 57-item test developed by Hans and Sybil Eysenck. The authors based this test on their studies of extraversion and neuroticism—the test yields a score for both of these traits as well as a "lie" score. The Eysenck Personality Inventory is derived from the Maudsley Medical Questionnaire and the Maudsley Personality Inventory, both of which were based on careful factor analysis of various sets of items. The Maudsley Personality Inventory was hailed as "an impressive achievement" in test development by Arthur Jensen (1965) in a review of the test in *The Sixth Mental Measurements Yearbook.* He noted that the traits of neuroticism and extraversion-introversion ("two relatively independent superfactors") account for most of the variance in the domain of personality. Neuroticism in this test (and in the E.P.I.) is defined in terms of emotional overresponsiveness, general emotional instability, and predisposition to neurotic breakdown under stress. Extraversion is equated with sociable, impulsive, uninhibited inclinations.

The test batteries—coded for group identification—were all taken by the members of the control group at home, whereas some of the members of the experimental group took the test batteries in the context of a group meeting and some took them at home. After the test batteries were returned to me, they were hand scored and the results were coded.

The resultant scores on the two inventories were combined to give a rating of psychological adjustment for each subject. The rating schema used in my study was adapted from one used in a study on the psychological adjustment of "overt male homosexuals." On my rating scale, the three categories of adjustment are:

A. *Superior to top adjustment:* Far better than the average person in the total population.

B. *As well adjusted as the average man in the total population:* nothing conspicuously good or bad.

C. *Bottom limit of normal group and/or maladjusted with signs of pathology.*

It should be emphasized that this combinatory rating was only a convenient summary score to compare global adjustment and was not intended to supersede the individual scales of the personality inventories. The responses to the self-report personality inventories, as manifested on the individual scales of these tests, along with the answers to the motivational questions and the adjustment rating for each subject, constituted the data of the experiment.

The Results

Strikingly, there were *no* significant differences in rated psychological adjustment between the groups of homosexually oriented and heterosexually oriented women (see Table 1).* Most of the women in each group could be characterized as well-functioning. Nor were the homosexually oriented women any more neurotic or variable in their psychological functioning than the heterosexually oriented control-group members. This finding is in direct contradiction to what most people (including most psychiatrists and psychologists) would have predicted.

Table 1

Psychological Adjustment Ratings Assigned to Experimental-Group and Control-Group Subjects

Rating	Experimental Group (%)	Control Group (%)
A	2	0
B	83	85
C	15	15
	100	100

*Complete statistical results of all aspects of this study may be found in Mark Freedman, *Homosexuality Among Women and Psychological Adjustment,* unpublished doctoral dissertation, 1967.

The most unexpected and impressive finding was that the homosexually oriented women were functioning significantly *better* psychologically in several areas: work adjustment and job satisfaction; inner-direction (that is, living by one's own values, with an internal locus of evaluation); valuing the same things in life that fully functioning or self-actualizing people do; living in the present, rather than being obsessed with the past or the future; spontaneity; acceptance of their own natural aggressive feelings; sensitivity of responsiveness to their own needs and feelings; and capacity for developing meaningful relationships with other people, unencumbered by exaggerated expectations and obligations.

It was also discovered that the homosexually oriented women were no less self-accepting than heterosexually oriented women. They did seem, however, to be more masculinely identified than the heterosexually oriented women—at least with respect to motivational patterns of work satisfaction and acceptance of aggressive feelings; they were more like men in these areas than was the control group (see Table 2). Nevertheless, the homosexually oriented women manifested genuinely female interests for the most part, especially in their preference for close interpersonal relations rather than sex *per se* and in their overall emphasis on deriving life satisfactions from human relationships.

Since the control group was significantly older than the experimental group, it was important to ascertain whether the age variable had an effect on psychological adjustment and thus biased the results of the study. (Psychological maturity is believed by many people to be directly related to chronological age.) Table 3 is a comparison of the psychological adjustment ratings and the age characteristics of the combined experimental and control groups. Since there is no significant difference in ratings between the older and younger subjects (as statistically determined by using a chi square test), it seems highly improbable that the subjects' ages were an important determinant of the psychological adjustment ratings they attained.

The variables of psychotherapeutic experience and educational background, like the age variable, were found to

Table 2

Comparison of Experimental and Control Groups in Frequency of Specific Items Listed on Motivation-Hygiene Questions

Things Looked for in a Job or Project*

Item	Experimental Group (%)	Control Group (%)
Having at least one close friend with whom I work	6	12
A chance to see a project through to its completion	28	52
Good salary	34	11
Receiving praise for my work	12	5
Challenging work	68	78
Clean and neat surroundings	1	6
A chance to advance in my organization	34	25
Other	16	11
Other	1	0
	200	200

*Two factors were requested, resulting in a total of 200% for each group.

Sources of Happiness on the Job

	Experimental Group (%)	Control Group (%)
My relations with other people on the job	40	72
Finally completing a project	22	33
The salary and/or benefits I was getting	9	8
Being recognized for doing a good job	41	28

Table 2 continued

Sources of Happiness on the Job, continued

	Experimental Group (%)	Control Group (%)
The nature of the job I was working on	52	47
The conditions of the place where I was working	3	3
Promotion to a better job	15	6
Other	18	3
Other	0	0
	200	200

Sources of Unhappiness on the Job

	Experimental Group (%)	Control Group (%)
My relations with other people on the job	35	46
Not being able to finish a project	21	38
The salary and/or benefits I was getting	16	0
Not being recognized for doing a good job	21	23
The nature of the job I was working on	40	55
The conditions of the place where I was working	17	13
Not being promoted when I deserved to be	18	9
Other	26	16
Other	6	0
	200	200

Table 2 continued

Sources of Happiness in Life

	Experimental Group (%)	Control Group (%)
My financial situation	10	17
Achievement on my job	21	21
My relations with other people	47	42
My sexual relations	19	6
My physical health	6	18
Being "caught up" in an interesting project	26	34
Being involved in learning new things	46	40
Getting a better position on my job or in an organization	8	3
Getting a new car	3	3
Buying new clothes	1	2
Other	12	12
Other	1	2
	200	200

Sources of Unhappiness in Life

	Experimental Group (%)	Control Group (%)
My financial situation	33	19
The nature of the job I was working on	28	24
My relations with other people	42	34
My sexual relations	14	14
My physical health	9	28
Not being promoted when I deserved to be	6	5
Being alone	34	33
Other	28	31
Other	6	12
	200	200

Table 3

Comparison of Psychological Adjustment Ratings and Age Characteristics of the Combined Groups

Rating	45 Years Old or Less (%)	46 Years Old or More (%)
A	2	0
B	84	83
C	14	17
	100	100

be unrelated to assigned psychological adjustment ratings, as shown in Table 4.

Another question regarding possible bias in test results is whether the relatively better performance of the homosexually oriented women on the Personal Orientation Inventory was due to their "faking good." This seems highly unlikely in view of the fact that it is extremely difficult to simulate self-actualization on this test. In fact, individuals who are intellectually aware of some of the components of self-actualization (through the study of psychology) but who are not self-actualizing score excessively high on the scales of

Table 4

Comparison of Psychological Adjustment Ratings with Psychotherapeutic Experience and Educational Background of the Combined Groups

	Adjustment Rating (%)	
	A&B	C
Psychotherapeutic Experience	86	14
No Psychotherapeutic Experience	87	13
High School Graduate or Less	83	17
Entered College and Above	87	13

the P.O.I., well above the scoring range that characterizes the truly self-actualizing person.

It should also be emphasized that the self-report personality inventories and the personal data sheets are vulnerable to the criticisms of all self-report inventories, particularly the criticisms revolving around the influence of differences in phenomenological (individualized) perceptions on test responses. It is also germane to consider that these inventories tap only certain aspects of psychological functioning and that other aspects must be assessed with different instruments (such as projective tests). Thus, this study is complementary to other studies that have used different techniques and instruments to investigate the psychological concomitants of homosexuality.

As summarized above, the results of this study suggest that women who engage in homosexual relations are, to a certain extent, different in their psychodynamics from women whose mode of adjustment is heterosexual. It appears that homosexually oriented women are either initially more independent and inner-directed, in the sense of inner-direction being a core aspect of personality, or else they develop this self-direction and independence as a reaction to societal pressures against their mode of sexuality. (There is no way to ascertain whether either one or the other, or both of these alternatives, is correct, given the data of this study.) There are, additionally, other differences between the members of the experimental and control groups that are probably attributable to differences in choice of sexual outlet. These may be either the reaction to societal pressures or core personality traits. In either case, it is noteworthy that the experimental group manifested attributes of self-actualizing people to a greater extent than did the control group, particularly in their feeling reactivity, existentiality, spontaneity, self-actualizing values, and inner-direction. These differences suggest that the members of the experimental group are more sensitive to their own needs and are more oriented to living in the present than are the members of the control group. It must be re-emphasized that these value orientations may well have been developed as a response to societal pressures. That possibility is strengthened by the finding of no significant differences between the groups in self-acceptance. In other words, the reaction to social attitudes about homosexuality among the members of the experimental group seems to be an increased self-awareness and sensitivity to their own needs rather than a lowered self-acceptance. (This is also consistent with the finding that the members of the experimental group were more candid and less defensive than the members of the control group, as manifested by their lower score on the Lie scale of the Eysenck Personality Inventory.)

As mentioned previously, there were differences in the degree to which the subjects were like men in their motivational patterns of work satisfaction and in their acceptance of aggression. The results suggest that women who engage in homosexual relations are more masculine in some of their personality characteristics than are hetero-sexually oriented women. This is consonant with the theore-tical and empirical investigations of individuals whose principal interpersonal sexual outlet is homosexual. It should be mentioned, however, that the differences in motivational patterns of work satisfactions may be due to other factors besides differences in masculine identification; that is, the members of the experimental group have more actual experience with the world of work than do the members of the control group (since most of the former group work for a living); also, members of the experimental group may be sublimating some of their basic human needs by being very oriented to achievement on the job. Nevertheless, it seems correct to say that masculine identification has been an important influence on the psychodynamics of the homo-sexually oriented women studied here.

Despite the more masculine characteristics shown by experimental group members, their performance on the personality inventories and on the personal data sheets was *predominantly feminine*. That is, one of the main differences between men and women in psychological functioning is the relative importance in their lives of interpersonal relations. As pointed out previously, women are much more oriented to other people as a source of life satisfactions than are men. In terms of sexuality, men concentrate on the *sexual* aspect of sexual relations, while women concentrate on the *interpersonal* or *love* aspects of their close relationships. These general trends were found to be true of both the experimental and the control group, particularly in their responses to the motivational questions concerning the sources of life satisfactions and dissatisfactions. Most behavioral scientists (particularly psychotherapists) hold interpersonal relations to be a mainstay of happiness in life. The results of this study revealed interpersonal relations to be an important source of happiness and unhappiness in life for both groups.

The overall findings suggest several conclusions about the psychological concomitants of homosexuality among women. The first is that there *are* qualitative differences in personality characteristics between homosexually oriented and heterosexually oriented women, at least in these groups. However, these differences do not detract from the ability of the women who have chosen a homosexual mode of adjustment to function effectively in society. This point is true whether we consider the value orientation of these women to be the result of core personality traits or reactions to societal pressures against their mode of sexuality. The apparently low level of classic neurotic symptoms in these women may be the result of the fact that they are "acting out" their anxieties in their sexual behavior pattern. However, since there is nothing about homosexual behavior intrinsically damaging or deleterious to psychological functioning, this possible "acting out" may not be as maladaptive as had been thought.

8

Levels and Types of Psychological Functioning

In this chapter, the relationship between homosexuality and psychological functioning is considered more explicitly and thoroughly than in the preceding chapters, which have considered only specific facets of this topic. The chapter begins with a review of the empirical findings about the topic and then presents a more theoretical examination.

The results of the empirical research studies described in the preceding chapters are, on the whole, positive about the relationship between homosexuality and psychological functioning. They demonstrate that most of the homosexually oriented individuals evaluated in the studies function as well as comparable groups of heterosexually oriented individuals; that their functioning typically could be characterized as normal; and that, in some cases, their functioning even approximates that of self-actualizing people. Cumulatively, these positive studies dealt with more than 600 homosexually oriented subjects, whereas the studies with negative or mixed results (Cattell and Morony; Doidge and Holzman) had only about 150 homosexually oriented subjects in all. Table 5 summarizes the major findings of each of the studies discussed above.

Table 5

Summary of Research Studies (Using Control Groups) on the Relationship Between Homosexuality and Psychological Functioning

Researcher and Date of Publication	Results
Hooker (1957)	No significant differences were found between the number of "homosexuals" and "heterosexuals" having an adjustment rating of "normal" or better. (Two-thirds of each group were assigned an adjustment rating of "normal" or better.)
Liddicott (1957)	The "Homosexual" group did not reveal any evidence of trends toward a psychopathic personality. A few highly neurotic individuals were found in both the experimental and control groups.
Armon (1960)	The majority of the "homosexual" women were as well-functioning as the members of the control group.
Chang and Block (1960)	The two groups of subjects did not differ significantly in their degree of self-acceptance or in regard to the kind of ego ideal toward which they aspired.
Doidge and Holzman (1960)	Only the "markedly homosexual" group gave evidence of disturbance; the "partly homosexual" group gave test results that closely approximated the results of the "heterosexual" control groups.
Cattell and Morony (1962)	"Homosexuals" resembled anxiety neurotics in their test performance on the 16PF test.

Table 5 continued

Research and Date of Publication	Results
Dean and Richardson (1964)	"Homosexual" subjects at a high level of intelligence and effective functioning are very similar to the test performance of a comparable "heterosexual" group, both groups being in the "normal" range in test performance.
Deluca (1966)	On the Rorschach, the "homosexuals" varied as much from each other as from the controls; there seems to be no causal relationship between homosexuality and pathological functioning.
Miller (1966)	No significant differences were found in rated psychological adjustment between incarcerated women who engaged in homosexual activities and those who did not.
Schofield (1966)	The differences in psychological functioning between "homosexual" and "heterosexual" groups were very small.
Freedman (1967)	Homosexually oriented women were as well-functioning, or better functioning, than a group of heterosexually oriented women.
Hopkins (1969)	In place of "neurotic," other, more positive terms were suggested as descriptive of the homosexually oriented women studied.
Saghir, et al. (1970 *a*)	Homosexually oriented men compared favorably with heterosexually oriented ones and were seen as functioning well despite slightly greater "disability" and life changes.

Table 5 continued

Researcher and Date of Publication	Results
Saghir, et al. (1970*b*)	Homosexually oriented women studied were able to achieve, adapt, and be productive citizens, and were only slightly more disturbed than the heterosexual control group.

Levels of Psychological Functioning

It is appropriate here to discuss the various possible *levels* of psychological functioning that may be associated with homosexuality. The levels considered will extend from the most debilitating, psychosis, to the most salubrious, self-actualization.

Psychosis. There have been several theories coupling homosexuality with some forms of psychosis. In particular, the different types of paranoia, paranoid state, and paranoid schizophrenia are thought to be caused, in part, by sexual conflict—especially by the inability to acknowledge homosexual impulses. The theories of the genesis of paranoia, in relation to homosexuality, are based entirely on psychoanalytic speculation. Since only in a minority of the cases of paranoia is homosexual *behavior* evident, and since psychoanalysis has been notoriously ineffective in eliminating or modifying this and other forms of psychosis, there is little basis to accept the psychoanalytic viewpoint on this subject.

Psychosis is characterized by lack of coping devices, inability to solve interpersonal problems, and general ineptness, all of which markedly reduce the interpersonal sexual experiences of the psychotic individual. In other words, sexual experiences, whether heterosexual or homosexual, are relatively rare in the psychotic individual's life, compared with a normally functioning individual.

There is no substantial evidence that there are more psychotic individuals among the population of homosexually oriented individuals than among the community of heterosexually oriented people.

Neurosis. Neurotic functioning has been investigated more thoroughly by psychologists and psychiatrists than any other level of functioning, including normal functioning. The most prevalent view of neurosis is in terms of emotional over-responsivity and inability to give and receive love.

The available research studies suggest that a slightly greater number of homosexually oriented than heterosexually oriented individuals manifest neurotic characteristics, although in both groups these individuals are far outnumbered by normally functioning ones. The tremendous societal pressure against homosexuality would seem to contribute to the genesis and maintenance of neurotic characteristics, just as the negative attitude of the majority has made some minority-group members, such as blacks and Jews, neurotic. On the other hand, societal pressure can also foster independence and inner-directedness in the victims of this pressure. Most neurotics are able to function effectively in many areas of their lives, particularly in those areas that are more technically and less people oriented. (An example of such a person is seen in the biography of Ruth Feld below.) It is important to remember that an individual's disorder is never a justification for blaming or for maintaining pressures against the individual; such attitudes only perpetuate the disorder.

Ruth Feld

Ruth Feld is a 32-year-old sociologist who works for the San Fernando city council in California. She is the eldest child in a family of four and was raised as a Jew (although she is now agnostic). Ruth was born in Poland but emigrated to the United States with her family when she was 14 years old.

After adjusting to American schools, Ruth began to excel in high school and graduated second in her class. She went on to one of the University of California schools, where she majored in sociology. Her graduate work was done at a private midwestern university that had awarded her a fellowship.

Ruth first became aware of attraction to girls when she was in grammar school in Poland. During high school, she had a crush on one of her teachers, but nothing ever came of that. She and her first-year roommate in college sometimes slept together and fondled each other, but the relationship never progressed to overt sexual activity. In retrospect, she sees their actions as an extension of their closeness and liking for each other. Her first sexual activity with a woman occurred when she was in graduate school: a close acquaintance initiated a touching, petting, and kissing sequence that culminated in her performing cunnilingus on Ruth. This was very pleasurable for Ruth, and she began a two-year relationship with this woman. The relationship fulfilled her needs for personal support, appreciation, and emotional contact as well as sex.

Although a pleasant person, Ruth is not physically attractive. Since her first affair broke up, she has had a hard time finding other partners. (She has never had sex with a man and has had few sexual encounters with women.) Her need for companionship and sex has made her feel desperate at times, so much so that she has been really intrusive in trying to make contact with other women and has made herself a pathetic figure. Another homosexually oriented woman, whom she was attracted to, was overwhelmed by phone calls and presents from Ruth; she was put off by Ruth's sad attempts to make contact rather than pleased or attracted to her.

Ruth is of superior intelligence, although she has poor social comprehension, which is reflected in her judgments of other people and of their interests and motivations. Professionally, she is doing well; personally, she has much growth, maturity, and social know-how to acquire. Because of these lacks as well as her unattractiveness, she will probably lead a solitary life with only sporadic encounters and relationships that are satisfying or fulfilling.

Whatever the level of the individual's functioning, sexual behavior in itself has little to do with determining that level of functioning. It is only the person's *attitude* toward his sexuality that can cause disturbance or conflict. (Consider all the guilt and shame both heterosexual and homosexual behaviors have caused people raised in puritanical society.) People who accept their own sexual behaviors without guilt or shame are less likely to manifest disturbance than are people who don't accept their own sexual behaviors, whether these behaviors be heterosexual or homosexual. Of course, society's condemnation of interpersonal sexual behaviors other than face-to-face heterosexual intercourse reinforces this guilt and shame. Since society is more negativistic about homosexual behavior than any other interpersonal sexual behaviors, this attitude in turn accounts for the greater guilt and shame among homosexually oriented individuals toward their sexuality. The ones who do not "work through" or resolve these attitudes, like Jack Main in the biography below, are more likely to exhibit neurotic functioning. Again, as stated above, only a *minority* of homosexually oriented individuals seem to be functioning at a neurotic level.

Jack Main

Jack Main is a 19-year-old student in a small business college in Albany, New York. He grew up as an only child in a household characterized by rigidity and intolerance. His parents were of a fundamentalist religious persuasion, and Jack learned early to lie and scheme in order to survive in this situation. His initial manipulation of his parents later extended to a perception of all people as objects to be manipulated in order to get his own way.

In high school, Jack's apathetic performance produced a mediocre record; when he graduated, he decided to "bum around" for awhile. But after a year of drifting he was pressured by his parents into enrolling at a business school.

Jack's homosexual activities started at the age of 13, when he engaged in mutual masturbation with a friend. When he was in high school, he had much sex with his peers as well as college students in the town whom he "cruised" in the park or on the street. Although he engages in a wide variety of homosexual activities, he is particularly fond of active partnership in fellatio. (He is excited about multiple sex, having engaged in numerous "three ways" and once in a "ten way" orgy.) Jack has never had sex with a woman, however.

At the age of 15, Jack began taking drugs such as marijuana, LSD, and cocaine. He takes them without apparent intellectual or aesthetic appreciation—merely for the experience. Curiously he has no desire for sex when he is on drugs.

Jack is of average intelligence. He has shallow affect and no deep personal or emotional relationships. People exist to be manipulated to his own purposes.

As a slim, pleasant looking, blond-haired young man, Jack's self-image is that of a boy, not a man, and he consequently prefers to have sex with younger men (usually 15 to 19 years old). He is attracted to the sensuality of sex—hence his preferences in bed.

Jack is still drifting. He has no real goals or abiding interests, just superficial activities such as dabbling in astrology and séances; he claims an attraction to Edgar Allan Poe's verse but really knows little about the author or his poetry. Jack is like many vacuous young men in the homosexual scene who have no interests or goals to give them direction, and who continue drifting in an aimless, irresponsible manner all their lives.

Psychopathy. In the psychiatric nomenclature, "character disorders" and "psychopathy" have been wastebasket categories in which to throw persons who did not exactly fit into other formal categories. In this way, homosexually oriented people were classified as psychopathic or as manifesting a character disorder. These categories are based on the concept that the individuals in the category are either amoral or immoral (better, asocial or antisocial). However, unlike Jack Main, most homosexually oriented individuals do not fit this description, unless you take these definitions literally to mean that because most homosexually oriented people are breaking the law by engaging in outlawed sexual behaviors, they are therefore immoral and antisocial. (Anyone who has ever known any homosexually oriented people understands that it is fatuous to conceive of all of these individuals as lacking conscience or a moral sense.)

People occasionally associate homosexuality with child molestation. This connection is not based on factual data, which report that a child molester's victim is as frequently a girl as it is a boy and that there is virtually no resemblance between the character and behavior of a child molester and that of a typical homosexually oriented person (Gebhard and associates, 1965). The vast majority of homosexually oriented people have no sexual interest in children, just as the majority of heterosexually oriented people do not.

Lack of conscience, most psychologists know, is not a group characteristic; amoral attitudes are distributed in the population in much the same way that intelligence is, in a more-or-less fashion. (Technically, this can be conceptualized by the bell-shaped curve.) Moreover, there is no evidence that there is a causal relationship between sexuality and amorality, in the sense that certain forms of sexuality *cause* or *promote* amoral behavior; deviant sexuality is, on the other hand, occasionally a consequence of an asocial mode of living.

Normality. Because of the pervasiveness of homosexual behavior in Western society, which Kinsey and other researchers have discovered, it appears that there is no *a priori* relationship between homosexual behavior and psychopathology or disturbed functioning. Rather, the question is whether homosexually oriented individuals are more disturbed in general than heterosexually oriented individuals. As we have seen in the research studies, the majority are not.

That some of the homosexually oriented population *are* more disturbed seems to be a result of the tremendous societal pressures against homosexuality. Some authorities have made much of this point. However, we tend to forget that people are *resilient* creatures, capable of coping with many pressures and much stress. This is why the functioning of most homosexually oriented individuals can be characterized as generally efficient, effective, and normal.

Self-actualization. As with the concept of normality, there are also many interpretations of the meaning of "self-actualization." Generally, the mainstays of this concept are the fulfilling of one's unique potentialities, self-acceptance, and the ability to have close interpersonal relationships. According to these criteria, at least as great a percentage of the homosexually oriented population is "self-actualizing" as of the heterosexually oriented population, although in both populations these people are relatively rare (at best only three per cent of the entire population). This conclusion has been corroborated by the empirical research studies on the relationship between homosexuality and psychological functioning.

It is precisely in the area of self-actualization that the distinction between psychological adjustment and psychological functioning arises. Adjustment implies fitting into the society and conventionality; self-actualization entails living by one's own values, although this does not preclude overt compliance with most of society's conventions. (The self-actualizing person may generally dress like other people and conform to many of society's mores and laws, but he has his own individual attitude and style with regard to more significant matters, such as sexuality or drinking or smoking marijuana, which he doesn't flaunt.) Many people today are frightened by the prospect of this type of individualism as manifested by the self-actualizing person. They fear that it will result in a state of anarchy or chaos in the society. The available evidence suggests a far different conclusion—that when individuals live their own lives and pursue their own destinies, the consequence is generally *productive activity in the social interest.* This conclusion is the result of theoretical and empirical investigation by such men as Abraham Maslow,

Carl Rogers, Erik Erickson, Frederick Herzberg, Paul
Goodman, and John W. Gardner.

Types of Functioning

Different *levels* of psychological functioning have
just been considered; now let us look at the different *types* of
functioning manifested by homosexually oriented individuals. There is no accurate way to assess how prevalent
each type of functioning is among the homosexually oriented
population, so speculation on the degree of prevalence would
be fruitless.

"The Homosexual." Some homosexually oriented
individuals accept the societal stereotype of "the homosexual" and consolidate their identity around this stereotype.
The facets of this stereotype which they accept, and act on,
are, for men, effeminacy, superficiality, promiscuity, and
maliciousness; for women, roughness, insensitivity, and domi-
nance. That this situation (consolidation of identity around
the societal stereotype) occurs is a product of an insidious
psychological phenomenon—the acceptance by members of a
minority group of society's evaluation of them and the
consequent engagement in the role that society has written
for them. Since society's evaluation of a given minority group
is multi-faceted, we see the facets of the stereotype as
dominant characteristics of different individuals. Thus, the
pushy Jew is as much a result of the stereotype as is the
mercenary Jew or the cunning Jew. And so is the shuffling
black or the sassy one. So with homosexually oriented people
who accept and act on the societal stereotype, we may see
one or more of the above-mentioned attributes in each
person. (The "effeminate homosexual" may also be malicious
or promiscuous, but not necessarily so.)

The most unfortunate part of this phenomenon is
the *waste* of potential that results from a person's subordi-
nating his uniqueness to act out a stereotype role with which
he has mistakenly identified. Also, the particular characteristics that are prominent in such a person's functioning—
such as those described in the biography of David Bond

below—are typically ones that diminish him and reduce the possibilities of leading a full, meaningful life. To glory in superficiality might be temporarily pleasing or delightful— "What a camp!"—but in the long run is deleterious to the experience of the richness of living.

David Bond

David Bond is a 26-year-old junior high school teacher in a San Francisco suburb. He is the younger of two children and comes from a midwestern Lutheran background. His father divorced his mother when David was in his teens, and the mother subsequently became an alcoholic. David's father seemed distant and cool to him as he was growing up, and his mother rejected him in subtle ways (this, at least, is David's perception of them). As a consequence, David's sense of self was always shaky, including his sexual identification. His slight effeminacy is probably a result of an attempt to reach out and be like his mother, who nonetheless did not relate to him.

In high school, David did respectably, and he went on to a state university in the midwest. There he earned a bachelor's degree with a teaching certificate for manual arts in junior and senior high school. David is very talented at draftsmanship and woodworking; he designs and builds furniture as a hobby. He has managed, through student and occupational deferments, to avoid military service.

David's self-identification as homosexual preceded any sexual activities. He first "came out" in the homosexual scene when he was at college, having sex with his roommate and subsequently going to gay bars in a nearby city. He feels shame about his sexual activities and still engages only in mutual masturbation, body rubbing, and passive partnership in fellatio. Recently, he has established a long-term relationship with another man, and his sexual repertoire will probably expand through the trust and give-and-take that usually accompanies a close personal relationship of that kind.

Socially, David is very gregarious and extro-
verted. He has many friends, and he enjoys parties
and other get-togethers a lot. Friendships represent
to him the closeness he never had with his parents.

David is a tall, slim young man with blond
hair and strikingly blue eyes. He is of bright-
average intelligence and has a capacity for close
relationships. However, his life is darkened by the
guilt he feels about his sexuality as well as by low
self-esteem despite all his strengths and positive
attributes. Although he was never close to his
parents, he desperately wanted his mother's attention and approval. Her drinking produced liver
dysfunction, which hospitalized her for many
months. When she died, David was visiting friends
in another city—in fact, he was at a homosexual
party the night she died. When he returned, he was
severely disturbed and felt tremendously guilty
(although he had regularly visited her during her
hospitalization). His guilty thoughts led him to
believe that he was really only "a worthless fag,"
and he consequently took on this role. David now
is the superficial "fairy": he glories in "camp"
humor and other trivia and his life revolves around
this self-concept. Unless he can be jarred out of his
self-contempt (by personal support from friends or
by psychotherapy), David will get along, suppres-
sing his real potential and living as he believes other
people think he should.

This type of functioning does exist. In fact, most
people in our society are cognizant of it precisely because it
derives from and is based on societal stereotypic thinking
about homosexuality. Most people are, unfortunately, not so
aware of the next two types of functioning to be discussed.

Pragmatism. Another type of functioning is
exemplified by the homosexually oriented individual who is
pragmatic in his approach to living. This person acknowledges
the dangers of being homosexually oriented in the society,
but he is willing and able to live effectively despite these
dangers. He maximizes the rewards and pleasures of living
and also manages the omnipresent social problems revolving

around homosexuality. Such a person is simultaneously a part of the society and an outsider abiding there. He disguises his sexual identity on his job, wearing the mask of heterosexuality there as well as in his interactions with most of the other persons he has to deal with in order to live. (He, like the vast majority of homosexually oriented people, is not outwardly identifiable by most people.) He befriends both heterosexually and homosexually oriented persons. And he learns how to fulfill his sexual needs most efficiently—how to find friends who will also be sexual partners, how to look and conduct himself in order to be successful in meeting people for social or sexual contacts, and so on. The quality that most characterizes him is his pragmatic outlook on life. This type of individual has the greatest chance of attaining a self-actualizing level of functioning, because he is typically attending to his psychological growth needs (generally through his work) and is also fulfilling his basic human needs, including sex, companionship, and comfortable environment.

Creative Oppositionalism. Creativity has been considered from various perspectives—as process, as product, and as statistic (frequency with which it appears in the population. The most appealing definition is Adrian Van Kaam's definition of creativity as "the productive use of past experience." But there is a phenomenon that differs from this type of creativity—one we can call "creative oppositionalism." This is a phenomenological perspective on the world that results in important creations, and which is the result of the reaction of societal pressures by certain individuals. This type of creativity usually manifests itself in sensitive, intelligent, and original members of a given minority group. Their talents foster the creativity, but it is the societal pressures that determine the form their creations take. That is, not only are their creations original, but they also represent unique reactions to fundamental trends or perspectives of the society that demeans or disdains "their kind." Thus, Martin Luther King, Jr., used his unique social genius to unite a wide diversity of people in order to gain the individual rights and liberties that up till then had been mostly American rhetoric. Had he been born in a society that did not discriminate against blacks, his creativity would probably have taken more conventional forms. Other black persons who have typified this mode of "creative oppositionalism" are Angela Davis, Dick Gregory, Eldridge Cleaver, and James Earl Jones. (Similarly, this type of functioning is manifested by many Jews in American society, from Philip Roth to Walter Lippmann, from Mark Rudd to Frieda Fromm-Reichmann, from Bob Dylan to Susan Sontag.)

In some respects one of the most harassed groups in our society, homosexually oriented individuals are also the source of this type of creativity. It is well known that homosexually oriented individuals have changed the shape of the theater, the novel, economics, modern dance, and social thinking in this century. Because of the dangers of society's wrath, most of these people have not permitted publicity about their sexual predispositions, except by word-of-mouth communication. That is why it is impossible to catalog their names, as has been done above with examples of Jews or blacks who manifest "creative oppositionalism." (Even the most dynamic living American playwright does not permit publicity about his sexual orientation. This is prototypic of the position taken by virtually all homosexually oriented persons who are creative and oppositional in their creations.) The only example that can be given here is of an individual who after his death was revealed to be homosexually oriented: John Maynard Keynes. It was Keynes' economic theories (now referred to as the New Economics) that reshaped economic policy and thinking in the United States, particularly during the Kennedy administration. Of course, only speculation can estimate to what extent Keynes' sexual predisposition provided the foundations for his original and oppositional thinking. (This relationship has been established clearly and unequivocally with respect to some homosexually oriented people who are alive and still creating, much as the relationship between discrimination and form of creative expression is clear with regard to Eldridge Cleaver or James Earl Jones. Certainly some of the Gay Liberation people, who advocate social reassessment of our attitudes to sex-roles and sexual behavior fall into this category.) It is in this type of functioning that the person experiences himself as the outsider abiding in the society most clearly. His creative oppositionalism renews and remakes the society.

There are surely other levels or types of psychological functioning associated with homosexuality, but it is impossible to encompass them here simply because we don't know what they all are yet.

9

Conclusions

Homosexuality is so diverse and complex that at any one time only selected aspects of it can be discussed in a meaningful way. I have attempted in this book to examine the relationship between homosexuality and psychological functioning, and have discussed the biological, sociological, statistical, and phenomenological aspects of homosexuality only as they pertain to this topic. I would like to review my conclusions here and to suggest new areas of investigation that will enhance our knowledge of this important topic.

The behavorial approach to homosexuality is more meritorious than the sickness approach. This behavioral approach contributes a realistic and parsimonious definition of homosexuality: sexual relations between members of the same sex. Such a definition avoids the artificial dichotomy of "the homosexual" and "the heterosexual" and acknowledges the inherent *pansexual* nature of man. The behavioral approach also establishes the social-learning basis for the sexual predispositions of homosexually oriented individuals and shows that the *only* precondition for homosexual behavior is an attraction to a member of the same sex (and that cross-sex identification and fear of the opposite sex are not prerequisites for homosexual bahavior). The behavioral approach also allows for the fact that there are many possible psychological concomitants of homosexuality and that sexual pattern alone does not determine psychological functioning. The biography of Alan Harper is a good example of this point.

Alan Harper

Alan Harper is a 24-year-old department store employee who works as the head of the men's clothing section in the downtown branch of the store in Cincinnati. He is an only child, the son of Lutheran parents.

Alan is the graduate of a junior college in Ohio. He joined his company after graduation. Alan decided that going into the service would pose too many problems in view of his sexual orientation; when his physical examination for the service arrived, he "checked the box" (indicated his homosexual orientation) and thereby disqualified himself from military service.

When he was 16 years old, Alan first acted on his homosexual impulses, having sex with one of his high school friends. In high school, he was extremely effeminate (due in part to an over-identification with his mother and an under-identification with his father and with men in general) and was typed by some of his classmates as a "fairy" as early as junior high school. In high school, Alan had only three or four dates (and those only for the high school proms), and his heterosexual experience never progressed beyond the petting stage. Since that time, he has never had any sexual experience with women, but has confined his interpersonal sexual activities to men. Alan is a very Aryan-looking person, with clear blue eyes, sandy blond hair, and fine features. He is medium height, with a slim build. Since high school, Alan has divested himself of most of his effeminate characteristics, so that neither his appearance nor his mannerisms suggest his sexual orientation.

Alan has had considerable sexual experience with a large number of men. He is very successful in finding partners in gay bars and homosexual parties. He enjoys sex and finds sexual relations with a wide range of partners stimulating. (To characterize him as promiscuous would be to put a negative evaluation on his life, which does not seem to be warranted; quite simply, he is enjoying life without harming other people or himself.) Alan engages in a number of sexual behaviors, depending on what his partner would like to do and on his mood. He engages in mutual masturbation, in active or passive partnership in fellatio, and in active or passive partnership in anal intercourse. (Although some of these behaviors disgusted him when he first tried them, they no longer bother him. He has accepted the simplistic slogan "If it feels good, do it.")

Like many homosexually oriented people, Alan is an agnostic (in much the same uncritical way that some people hold a religious belief in God). He does not see the relevance of religion for his life now, and lives mostly in the present without being burdened by the past or obsessed with the future.

On the Wechsler Adult Intelligence Scale, Alan scored in the normal range of intelligence. He did better on the performance part of the test than on the verbal part, showing more manual dexterity than verbal facility. Alan evinced a slight neuroticism on a personality inventory, but not enough to interfere with his functioning. His performance on the tests was also characterized by extraversion and considerable narcissism. In fact, he manifests a great deal of egotism. (This is probably due to his consciousness of his good looks as well as to his success in finding sexual partners.) On the other hand, Alan has a remarkable zest for living, as well as a skill for enjoyable interpersonal relationships. He could be characterized as normal, not because he is average or typical but because of the good quality of his mental life and psychological functioning.

Good psychological functioning should not be defined in terms of sexual pattern but rather in terms of environmental mastery. The people who are most efficient in their psychological functioning are those who fulfill both their psychological growth needs (motivators) and their basic replenishment needs (hygiene-factors) of food, shelter, sex, companionship, status, and so on. Fulfillment of these needs is a matter of degree (more/less) rather than one of kind (either/or). This perspective on positive psychological functioning neither glorifies nor disregards sex, but realistically appraises the part sexuality plays in the totality of a person's life. And it sees positive psychological functioning as potentially within reach of most people in the population, regardless of sexual pattern.

Empirical psychological research has proved that homosexuality is compatible with positive psychological functioning. This statement is based on research studies with a large number of subjects in many geographic locales, using a wide variety of psychological instruments and techniques. These studies suggest that most homosexually oriented persons (who are generally not visible to us as such) are pragmatic in outlook, are coping efficiently with their life situations and are effective in environmental mastery. Many homosexually oriented individuals are, in fact—like Diane Miller in the biography below—self-actualizing.

Diane Miller

Diane Miller is a 22-year-old graduate student in creative writing at a Boston university. Diane is the second child of middle-class Jewish parents living in the New York metropolitan area. She was precocious as a child and excelled in her school work. Her undergraduate training was done at one of the Seven Sister colleges in New England.

Diane is pretty and looks almost fragile, with large brown eyes, a small nose and mouth, high cheekbones, and long dark-brown hair. She is about 5 feet 6 inches tall and is very lithe, wearing clothes that accentuate this feature. Being attractive, Diane was frequently asked out on dates in high school and college. Her dating experiences in high school were relatively pleasant for her, and she was stimulated by the petting experiences, but she would never engage in sexual intercourse. When she got to college, Diane was asked to go for a "big weekend" to an Eastern men's college; she did go, and had a sexual experience that was aversive to her because of the drinking and excitement of the event. After that time, she stopped accepting invitations to dances, dinner, or "weekends." (It was relatively easy to do this at her college, although she was typed as a "grind" by the girls for whom the social life was the biggest part of college.) She invested all her time and energy thereafter in school work, which resulted in an excellent grade-point average as well as some high-quality writing. These credits helped her get accepted to the creative writing program of an important university. At this university, she met another student who befriended her, and with whom she had her first homosexual experiences. The two of them have lived together for a year, and Diane has been happy with a social, intellectual, and sexual companion. (Her friend complements her intelligence and interests—she is a graduate student in sociology.)

Diane is a sensitive girl, but she is able to channel this sensitivity into her writing; she experiences the nuances of life and is not neurotically or masochistically sensitive. In her performances on psychological tests, her outstanding characteristics were related to existentiality, capacity for intimate contact, and feeling reactivity. She scored low on a measure of extraversion as well as on a measure of neuroticism. Her performance on the Wechsler Adult Intelligence Scale put her in the "superior" range of intellectual functioning.

Diane finds sexual relations *per se* secondary to personal relationships. She has only three or four friends, but they are close friends and not acquaintances. Two of them are male graduate students who have been able to accept the idea of a close personal relationship with her, involving the sharing of happy times, insights, and confidences, without demanding sex from her. Diane and her roommate enjoy fondling and sexual foreplay especially, and also engage in mutual masturbation; neither of them has engaged in cunnilingus.

Diane is not particularly attracted to the idea of marriage, despite pressure from her parents to marry and settle down. She enjoys the relationship she now has with her roommate and is not interested in having a family or a bland suburban existence. She is adept at writing, which she loves; this pursuit has assumed an importance for her that outweighs considerations of marriage or of anything that could tie down her life. She knows realistically that her present relationship with her roommate may not last forever, because of personal or financial factors; a dissolution of the relationship would make her unhappy, but it is secondary to her writing. She would try to find a similar relationship if this one dissolved, because of its rewards.

Diane is sensitive and has insight: a person who can transpose her perceptions and experience to high-quality writing. In terms of fulfilling her need for psychological growth and her basic human needs such as sex and companionship, Diane can be characterized as self-actualizing.

Needs for the Future

Probably the greatest need in the behavorial sciences now is for the evolution of a *workable* psychological definition of normality—one that will be acceptable both to professionals in this field and to the public. The medical-statistical definition of normality has been popular until recently, but certain researchers have caused discomfort by questioning the reality and the efficacy of this approach. A *workable* psychological definition of normality must perform two functions. First, it must correspond fairly closely to the reality of living; second, it must guide us in decisions of what phenomena to modify, because of radically self-destructive disharmony, and what phenomena to accept as part of the diversity and richness of life. I think the most workable psychological definition of normality is suggested by the "motivation-hygiene" theory. But this theory will not be acceptable to everyone—perhaps not even to the majority of people.

The area of motivational patterns as related to psychological growth needs and to other basic human needs (physiological and social) is a burgeoning one, but it still needs more research. Tentatively, the findings suggest that we have taken the wrong approach insofar as we have rigidly believed that all positive achievements derive from difficulties with sexuality and aggression. We are now discovering that positive achievement cannot be explained away in terms such as "sublimation" and "over-compensation." Similarly, the differentiation between psychological growth needs and other basic human needs is of great interest. Insight into this relationship will clarify the effects of motivation on sexuality and vice versa.

We also would do well to investigate how societal pressures (legal, moral, social) evoke widely divergent reactions such as self-hatred and increased self-direction (inner-directedness). If we can discover the connection, we will have a better understanding of social psychology and individual phenomenology.

One Last Comment

Implicit in this book is the idea that, with regard to sexuality, people should be allowed to engage in any behavior that does not directly harm others. This attitude has been accepted into the legal systems of Great Britain, Holland, and Canada, but not as yet into American law. Of course, social attitudes to sexuality have to be changed as well, or else an atmosphere of fear, negation, and restrictiveness will continue to pervade society. Some theorists—notably Marshall McLuhan—maintain that the world is rapidly changing because of the speed of communication fostered by the electronics media and that these changes include a new tolerance for, and interest in *differentness*. This appreciation of differentness includes acceptance of people formerly discriminated against according to social, ethnic, religious, and sexual distinctions. Hopefully, then, a new climate of respect for diversity and acceptance of individual differences is arriving. With human relationships still resulting in individual chaos because of these divisions and discriminations, I hope this change arrives soon.

References

Adler, A. *Social Interest*. New York: Putnam, 1939.

Allport, G. W. *Pattern and Growth in Personality*. New York: The Commonwealth Fund, 1941.

Allport, G. W. *Becoming*. New Haven: Yale University Press, 1965.

Anastasi, A. *Psychological Testing*. New York: Macmillan, 1961.

Anderson, R. *Tea and Sympathy*. New York: Random House, 1953.

Angyal, A. *Foundations for a Science of Personality*. New York: The Commonwealth Fund, 1941.

Armon, V. "Some Personality Variables in Overt Female Homosexuality," *Journal of Projective Techniques*, *24* (1960), 292-309.

Arnold, M. B., and Gasson, J. A. *The Human Person*. New York: Ronald Press, 1954.

Baldwin, J. *Giovanni's Room*. New York: Dial, 1956.

Baldwin, J. *Another Country*. New York: Dial, 1962.

Barron, F. "The Disposition toward Originality," *Journal of Abnormal and Social Psychology*, *51* (1955), 478-485.

Barron, F. "Originality in Relation to Personality and Intellect," *Journal of Personality*, *25* (1957), 730-742.

Barron, F. "The Psychology of Imagination," *Scientific American, 199* (1958), 150-166.

Bergler, E. *Homosexuality: Disease or Way of Life?* New York: Hill and Wang, 1956.

Bieber, I. (Ed.). *Homosexuality, A Psychoanalytic Study.* New York: Basic Books, 1962.

Brown, D. "The Development of Sex-Role Inversion and Homosexuality," *Journal of Pediatrics, 60* (1957), 613-619.

Bühler, C. "Theoretical observations about life's basic tendencies," *American Journal of Psychotherapy, 13* (1959), 561-581.

Cattell, R., and Morony, J. H. "The Use of the 16PF in Distinguishing Homosexuals, Normals, and General Criminals," *Journal of Consulting Psychology, 26,* 6 (1962), 531-540.

Chang, J., and Block, J. "A Study of Identification in Male Homosexuals," *Journal of Consulting Psychology, 24,* 8 (1960), 307-310.

Churchill, W. *Homosexual Behavior among Males.* New York: Basic Books, 1967.

Cofer, C. N., and Appley, M. H. *Motivation: Theory and Research.* New York: Wiley, 1964.

Cohen, A. K. "The Study of Social Disorganization and Deviant Behavior," in R. Merton (Ed.), *Sociology Today.* New York: Basic Books, 1959.

Cory, D. W. *The Homosexual in America.* New York: Greenberg, 1951.

Cory, D. W. *The Lesbian in America.* New York: Citadel, 1964.

Crowley, M. *The Boys in the Band.* New York: Noonday, 1968.

Curran, D., and Parr, D. "Homosexuality: An Analysis of 100 Male Cases Seen in Private Practice," *British Medical Journal,* April 6, 1957.

Davids, A., *et al.* "Rorschach and T.A.T. Indices of Homosexuality in Overt Homosexuals, Neurotics, and Normal Males," *Journal of Abnormal Psychology, 53* (1956), 161-172.

Davidson, H. A. *Mental Hygiene,* 51, 5 (1967).

Dean, R. B., and Richardson, H. "Analysis of MMPI Profiles of 40 College-Educated Overt Male Homosexuals," *Journal of Consulting Psychology, 28* (1964), 483-486.

Deluca, J. "The Structure of Homosexuality," *Journal of Projective Techniques and Personality Assessment, 30,* 2 (1966), 187-191.

Deutsch, M. *Neuroses and Character Types.* New York: International Universities Press, 1964.

Dingwall, E. "Homosexuality through the Ages," in I. Rubin (Ed.), *The Third Sex.* New York: New Book Co., 1961.

Doidge, W., and Holzman, W. "Implications of Homosexuality among Air Force Trainees," *Journal of Consulting Psychology, 24* (1960), 9-13.

Drevdahl, J. E. "Factors of Importance for Creativity," *Journal of Clinical Psychology, 12* (1956), 23-26.

Drevdahl, J. E., and Cattell, R. B. "Personality and Creativity in Artists and Writers," *Journal of Clinical Psychology, 14* (1958), 107-111.

Dyer, C. *Staircase.* New York: Grove, 1968.

Ellis, A. *Homosexuality: Its Causes and Cure.* New York: Lyle Stuart, 1956.

Ellis, A. "A Homosexual Treated with Rational Psychotherapy," *Journal of Clinical Psychology, 15* (1959), 338-343.

Ellis, A. *The American Sexual Tragedy.* New York: Lyle Stuart, 1962.

Ellis, A. "The Effectiveness of Psychotherapy with Individuals Who Have Severe Homosexual Problems," in H. Ruitenbeek (Ed.), *The Problems of Homosexuality in Modern Society.* New York: Dutton, 1963.

Ellis, A. *Sex and the Single Man.* New York: Lyle Stuart, 1965.

Ellis, H. *Studies in the Psychology of Sex.* New York: Random House, 1936.

Erikson, E. "Identity and the life cycle," *Psychological Issues, 1* (1959), 18-171.

Erikson, E. *Identity: Youth and Crisis.* New York: Norton, 1967.

Eysenck, H. *Behavior Therapy and the Neuroses.* London: Pergamon Press, 1960.

Eysenck, H. *The Maudsley Personality Inventory.* San Diego: Educational and Industrial Testing Service, 1962.

Eysenck, H., and Eysenck, S. *The Eysenck Personality Inventory.* San Diego: Educational and Industrial Testing Service, 1963.

Feldman, M., and MacCulloch, M. "The Application of Anticipatory Avoidance Learning to the Treatment of Homosexuality," *BRAT, 2* (1965), 165-183.

Ford, C. S., and Beach, F. *Patterns of Sexual Behavior.* New York: Harper, 1951.

Frankl, V. "Beyond Self-Actualization and Self-Expression," *Journal of Existential Psychiatry, 1* (1960), 5-20.

Freedman, M. "Homosexuality among Women and Psychological Adjustment," *The Ladder, 12,* 2 (1968), 2-3.

Freud, S. *Three Contributions to the Theory of Sex.* Translated by A. A. Brill. New York: Nervous and Mental Disease Publishing Company, 1930.

Freund, K. "Treatment of Homosexuality," in H. J. Eysenck (Ed.), *Behaviour Therapy and the Neuroses.* London: Pergamon Press, 1960.

Freund, K. "A Laboratory Method for Diagnosing Predominance of Homo- or Hetero-Erotic Interest in the Male," *BRAT, 1* (1963), 85-93.

Friedan, B. *The Feminine Mystique.* New York: Norton, 1963.

Fromm, E. "Individual and Social Origins of Neurosis," *American Sociological Review, 9* (1944), 380-384.

Fromm, E. *The Art of Loving.* New York: Harper, 1956.

Fromm, E., and Elonen, A. "Projective Techniques in a Case of Female Homosexuality," *Journal of Projective Techniques, 15* (1951), 185-210.

Gardner, J. W. *Excellence.* New York: Harper and Row, 1961.

Gardner, J. W. *Self-Renewal.* New York: Harper and Row, 1964.

Gebhard, P., Gagnon, J., Pomeroy, W. and Christenson, C. *Sex Offenders.* New York: Harper, 1965.

Genet, J. *Our Lady of the Flowers.* New York: Grove, 1963.

Genet, J. *The Thief's Journal.* New York: Grove, 1964.

Ginott, H. G. *Between Parent and Child.* New York: Macmillan, 1965.

Gleuck, S. "The Home, the School and Delinquency," *Harvard Educational Review, 23* (1953), 17-32.

Gold, S., and Neurfeld, I. L. "A Learning Approach to the Treatment of Homosexuality," *BRAT, 2* (1965), 201-204.

Goldstein, K. *The Organism.* New York: American Book Co., 1939.

Goodman, P. *Growing Up Absurd*. New York: Random House, 1960.

Green, M. R. (Ed.). *Interpersonal Analysis: The Selected Papers of Clara M. Thompson*. New York: Basic Books, 1962.

Gross, A. *Strangers in Our Midst*. Washington: Public Affairs Press, 1962.

Grossack, M. M., Armstrong, T. and Lussieu, G. "Correlates of Self-Actualization," *Journal of Humanistic Psychology, 6* (1966), 87-88.

Group for the Advancement of Psychiatry, Committee on Cooperation with Governmental (Federal) Agencies. *Report on Homosexuality with Particular Emphasis on This Problem in Governmental Agencies* (Rep. No. 30). New York: 1965.

Guilford, J. P. "Creativity," *American Psychologist, 5* (1950), 444-454.

Hadfield, J. A., "The Cure of Homosexuality," *British Medical Journal, 1* (1958), 1323-1326.

Hall, C. S., and Lindzey, G. *Theories of Personality*. New York: Wiley, 1957.

Hall, R. *The Well of Loneliness*. New York: Pocket Books, 1959.

Havinghurst, R. J., and Neugarten, B. L. *Society and Education*. Boston: Allyn and Bacon, Inc., 1962.

Havinghurst, R. J., and Taba, H. *Adolescent Character and Personality*. New York: Wiley, 1949.

Hellman, L. *The Children's Hour*. New York: New American Library (Signet), 1962.

Hellman, R. J. "The Necessary and Sufficient Conditions of Creativity," *Journal of Humanistic Psychology, 3* (1963), 14-27.

Hemphill, R. E. "A Factual Study of Male Homosexuality," *British Medical Journal, 1* (1958), 1317-1323.

Herzberg, F. *Work and the Nature of Man*. Cleveland: World, 1966.

Herzberg, F., and Hamlin, R. "A Motivation-Hygiene Concept of Mental Health," *Mental Hygiene, 45* (1961), 394-401.

Herzberg, F., and Hamlin, R. "The Motivation-Hygiene Concept and Psychotherapy," *Mental Hygiene, 47* (1963), 384-397.

Herzberg, F., Mausner, B., and Snyderman, B. *The Motivation to Work*. New York: Wiley, 1959.

Hirschfeld, M. *Sexual Pathology*. New York: Julien Press, 1940.

Hoffman, M. *The Gay World*. New York: Basic Books, 1968.

Hooker, E. "The Adjustment of the Male Overt Homosexual," *Journal of Projective Techniques, 21* (1957), 18-31.

Hooker, E. "Male Homosexuality in the Rorschach," *Journal of Projective Techniques, 22* (1958), 33-54.

Hooker, E. "Symposium on Current Aspects of the Problems of Validity: What Is a Criterion?," *Journal of Projective Techniques, 23* (1959), 278-281.

Hopkins, J. "The Lesbian Personality," *British Journal of Psychiatry, 115*, 529 (1969), 1433-1436.

Horney, K. *Neurosis and Human Growth*. New York: Norton, 1958.

Horowitz, M. "The Homosexual's Image of Himself," *Mental Hygiene, 48* (1964), 197-201.

Isherwood, C. *A Single Man.* Simon and Schuster, 1964.

Jackson, D. D. *The Etiology of Schizophrenia*. New York: Basic Books, 1960.

Jahoda, M. *Current Concepts of Positive Mental Health*. New York: Basic Books, 1959.

James, B., "A Case of Homosexuality Treated by Aversion Therapy," *British Medical Journal, 1* (1962), 768-770.

Jensen, A. In O. Buros (Ed.), *The Sixth Mental Measurements Yearbook*. Highland Park: Gryphon Press, 1965.

Jersild, A. T. *Child Psychology*. Englewood Cliffs, N. J.: Prentice-Hall, Inc., 1960.

Jones, L. *The Toilet*. New York: Grove, 1964.

Jourard, S. *The Transparent Self*. New York: Van Nostrand, 1964.

Jung, C. G. *Modern Man in Search of a Soul*. New York: Harcourt, Brace, 1933.

Kallmann, F. J. "A Comparative Twin Study on the Genetic Aspects of Male Homosexuality," *Journal of Nervous and Mental Disorders, 115* (1952), 283-298.

Kent, C. In B. Murstein (Ed.), *Handbook of Projective Techniques.* New York: Basic Books, 1964.

Kimble, G. *Hilgard and Marquis' Conditioning and Learning.* New York: Appleton-Century-Crofts, 1961.

King, C. D. "The Meaning of Normal," *Yale Journal of Biology and Medicine, 17* (1945), 493-501.

Kinsey, A. *et al. Sexual Behavior in the Human Male.* Philadelphia: Saunders, 1948.

Kinsey, A. *et al. Sexual Behavior in the Human Female.* Philadelphia: Saunders, 1953.

Klaf, F. S. "Homosexuality and Paranoid Schizophrenia: A Survey of 150 Cases and Controls," *American Journal of Psychiatry, 116* (1960), 1070-1075.

Krafft-Ebing, R. von. *Psychopathia Sexualis.* Brooklyn: Physicians and Surgeons Book Co., 1886.

Leib, J. W. and Snyder, W. V. "Effects of Group Discussions on Underachievement and Self-Actualization," *Journal of Counseling Psychology, 14* (1967), 282-285.

Leuba, C. *The Sexual Nature of Man.* New York: Doubleday, 1954.

Lewin, K. "Behavior and Development as a Function of the Total Situation," in L. Carmichael (Ed.), *Manual of Child Psychology.* New York: Wiley, 1946.

Liddicoat, R. Untitled article in *British Medical Journal,* 1957, 1110-1111.

Lindzey, G. "Seer versus Sign," *Journal of Experimental Research in Personality, 1* (1965), 17-26.

Lorr, M., and Jenkins, R. L. "Three Factors in Parent Behavior," *Journal of Consulting Psychology, 17* (1953), 306-308.

Lynd, H. M. *On Shame and the Search for Identity.* New York: Harcourt, Brace, 1958.

Machover, S. "Clinical and Objective Studies of Personality Variables in Alcoholism, III. An Objective Study of Homosexuality in Alcoholism," *Quarterly Journal of Studies on Alcohol, 20* (1959), 528-542.

MacKinnon, D. W. "The Nature and Nurture of Creative Talent," *American Psychologist, 17* (1962), 383-395.

Magee, B. *One in Twenty.* New York: Doubleday, 1965.

MaGuire, R. J., and Vallence, M., "Aversion Therapy by Electric Shock: A Simple Technique," *British Medical Journal, 1* (1964), 151-153.

MaGuire, R. J., and Carlisle, J. M. "Sexual Deviations as Conditioned Behavior: A Hypothesis," *BRAT, 2* (1965), 185-190.

Marcus, F. *The Killing of Sister George.* New York: Random House, 1967.

Marmor, J. (Ed.). *Sexual Inversion.* New York: Basic Books, 1965.

Maslow, A. H. *Motivation and Personality*. New York: Harper, 1954.

Maslow, A. H. "A Philosophy of Psychology," in J. Fairchild (Ed.), *Personal Problems and Psychological Frontiers*. New York: Sheridan House Press, 1957.

Maslow, A. H. *Toward a Psychology of Being*. Princeton, N. J.: Van Nostrand, 1962.

Maslow, A. H. *Religions, Values, and Peak Experiences*. Columbus: Ohio State University Press, 1964.

Max, L. "Breaking Up a Homosexual Fixation by the Conditioned Reaction Technique," *Psychological Bulletin, 32* (1935), 734.

May, R. *Man's Search for Himself*. New York: Norton, 1953.

McLuhan, M. *Understanding Media*. New York: McGraw-Hill, 1964.

McNemar, Q. *Psychological Statistics*. New York: Wiley, 1962.

Mead, M. *Sex and Temperament in Three Primitive Societies*. New York: Morrow, 1935.

Mensh, I. "Psychopathic Condition, Addictions and Sexual Deviations," in B. Wolman (Ed.), *Handbook of Clinical Psychology*. New York: McGraw-Hill, 1965.

Miller, A. *A View from the Bridge*. New York: Viking, 1955.

Miller, W. G. "Characteristics of Homosexually Involved Incarcerated Females," *Journal of Consulting Psychology, 30* (1966), 193-198.

Milton, O. (Ed.). *Behavior Disorders*. New York: Lippincott, 1965.

Moustakas, C. *Creativity and Conformity*. Princeton, N. J.: Van Nostrand, 1967.

Mummery, D. V. "Family Backgrounds of Assertive and Non-assertive Children," *Child Development, 25* (1954), 63-80.

Nitsche, C. J.,*et al.* "Homosexuality and the Rorschach," *Journal of Consulting Psychology, 20* (1956), 196-199.

Nuttin, J. "Intimacy and Shame in the Dynamic Structure of Personality," in M. L. Reymert (Ed.), *Feelings and Emotions*. New York: McGraw-Hill 1950.

Nuttin, J. *Psychoanalysis and Personality*. New York: Sheed and Ward, 1953.

Offer, D., and Sabshin, M. *Normality*. New York: Basic Books, 1966.

Panton, J. H. "A New MMPI Scale for the Identification of Homosexuality," *Journal of Clinical Psychology, 16* (1960), 17-21.

Peck, R. F., Havighurst, R. J., Cooper, R., Lilienthal, J., and Moore, D. *The Psychology of Character Development.* New York: Wiley, 1960.

Perls, F., Hefferline, R. E., and Goodman, P. *Gestalt Therapy.* New York: Julian Press, 1951.

Pomeroy, W. "What Is Normal?," *Playboy*, March 1965, 97.

Purdy, J. *Eustace Chisholm and the Works.* New York: Farrar, Straus and Giroux, 1967.

Querlin, M. *Women without Men.* New York: Dell, 1965.

Rachman, S., "Sexual Disorders and Behavior Therapy," *American Journal of Psychiatry, 118* (1961), 235-240.

Rechy, J. *City of Night.* New York: Grove, 1963.

Rechy, J. *Numbers.* New York: Grove, 1967.

Renault, M. *The Charioteer.* New York: Pantheon, 1959.

Riesman, D., with Glazer, N., and Denney, R. *The Lonely Crowd.* New Haven: Yale University Press, 1950.

Rogers, C. R. "A Theory of Therapy, Personality and Interpersonal Relationships, as Developed in the Client-Centered Framework," in S. Koch (Ed.), *Psychology: A Study of a Science*, Volume III. New York: McGraw-Hill, 1959.

Rogers, C. R. "The Concept of the Fully Functioning Person," *Psychotherapy, 1* (1963), 17-26.

Rogers, C. R., and Dymond, R. F. (Eds.), *Psychotherapy and Personality Change.* Chicago: University of Chicago Press, 1954.

Rubin, I. (Ed.). *The Third Sex.* New York: New Book Co., 1961.

Ruitenbeek, H. *The Problem of Homosexuality in Modern Society.* New York: Dutton, 1963.

Saghir, M., and Robins, E. "Homosexuality: I. Sexual Behavior of the Human Female," *Archives of General Psychiatry, 20* (February 1969).

Saghir, M., *et al.* "Homosexuality: III. Psychiatric Disorders and Disability in the Male Homosexual," *American Journal of Psychiatry , 126*, 8 (1970), 1079-1086. (*a*)

Saghir, M., *et al.* "Homosexuality: IV. Psychiatric Disorders in the Female Homosexual," *American Journal of Psychiatry, 127*, 2 (1970), 147-154. (*b*)

Sanford, N. "The Dynamics of Identification," *Psychology Review, 62* (1955), 106-118.

Sartre, J. P. *No Exit.* New York: Knopf, 1947.

Satir, V. *Conjoint Family Therapy.* Palo Alto: Science and Behavior Books, Inc., 1964.

Schachtel, E. G. *Metamorphosis.* New York: Basic Books, 1959.

Schofield, M. *A Minority; a Report on the Life of the Male Homosexual in Great Britain.* London: Longmans, 1960.

Schofield, M. *Sociological Aspects of Homosexuality.* New York: Little, Brown, 1966.

Schofield, W. *Psychotherapy: The Purchase of Friendship.* New York: Prentice-Hall, 1964.

Schultz, K. V. "The Psychologically Healthy Person: A Study in Identification and Prediction," *Journal of Clinical Psychology, 14* (1958), 112-117.

Shostrom, E. *The Personal Orientation Inventory.* San Diego: Educational and Industrial Testing Service, 1963.

Shostrom, E. "An Inventory for the Measurement of Self-Actualization," *Educational and Psychological Measurement, 24* (1964), 207-218.

Shostrom, E. *Man the Manipulator.* Nashville: Abingdon, 1967.

Siegel, S. *Non-parametric Statistics.* New York: McGraw-Hill, 1956.

Sinnot, E. W. "The Biology of Purpose," *American Journal of Orthopsychiatry, 22* (1952), 457-468.

Staats, A., and Staats, C. *Complex Human Behavior.* New York: Holt, Rinehart and Winston, 1964.

Stearn, J. *The Sixth Man.* New York: Doubleday, 1961.

Stearn, J. *The Grapevine.* New York: Doubleday, 1964.

Stevenson, I., and Wolpe, J. "Recovery from Sexual Deviations through Overcoming Nonsexual Neurotic Responses," *American Journal of Psychiatry, 116* (1960), 737-742.

Sullivan, H. S. *The Interpersonal Theory of Psychiatry.* New York: Norton, 1953.

Szasz, T. "The Myth of Mental Illness," in O. Milton (Ed.), *Behavior Disorders.* New York: Lippincott, 1965.

Thorpe, J. G. and Schmidt, E., "Therapeutic Failure in a Case of Aversion Therapy," *BRAT, 1* (1963), 293-296.

Thorpe, J. G., Schmidt, E., and Castell, D., "A Comparison of Positive and Negative (Aversive) Conditioning in the Treatment of Homosexuality," *BRAT, 1* (1963), 357-362.

Trilling, L. "The Kinsey Report," in D. P. Geddes (Ed.), *An Analysis of the Kinsey Reports.* New York: New American Library (Mentor), 1954.

Tripp, C. A. "Who Is a Homosexual?," *The Ladder, 10,* 3 (1965), 15-23.

Vidal, G. *The City and the Pillar.* New York: Dutton, 1965.

Walsh, W. B "Validity of Self-Report," *Journal of Counseling Psychology, 14* (1967), 18-23.

Watson, G. "Some Personality Differences in Children Related to Strict or Permissive Parental Discipline," *Journal of Psychology, 44* (1957), 227-249.

Watts, A. "Circle of Sex," *Playboy*, December 1965, 135.

West, L. J., *et al.* "An Approach to the Problem of Homosexuality in Military Service," *American Journal of Psychiatry, 115* (1958), 392-401.

Wheeler, W. "Analysis of Rorschach Indices of Male Homosexuality," *Rorschach Research Exchange, 13* (1949), 97-126.

White, R. W. *Lives in Progress.* New York: Holt, Rinehart and Winston, 1952.

White R. W. "Motivation Reconsidered: The Concept of Competence," *Psychological Review, 66* (1959), 297-338.

Wilde, O. *The Picture of Dorian Gray.* New York: New American Library (Signet), 1962.

Williams, T. *Cat on a Hot Tin Roof.* New York: New Directions, 1955.

Williams, T. *Suddenly Last Summer.* New York:New Directions, 1958.

Wolfenden, Sir John. *Report of the Committee on Homosexual Offenses and Prostitution.* London: Her Majesty's Stationery Office, 1957.

Wolpe, J. "Reciprocal Inhibition," in H. J. Eysenck (Ed.), *Behavior Therapy and the Neuroses.* London: Pergamon Press, 1960.

Yamahiro, R. S., *et al.* "Validity of Two Indices of Sexual Deviancy," *Journal of Clinical Psychology, 16* (1960), 21-24.

Index